STRING
TOO SHORT TO
BE SAVED

Also by Donald Hall

STRING
TOO SHORT TO BE
SAVED

Recollections of Summers
on a New England Farm

Donald Hall

GODINE • BOSTON • 2021

First published in 1979 by GODINE
Boston, Massachusetts

Excerpts from this book appeared in *The American Scholar* and *Audience*.
Two chapters, "The Wild Heifers" and "The Blueberry Picking"
(under the title "A Day on Ragged"), first appeared in *The New Yorker*.
Portions of the Epilogue appeared in *Ford Times*.

LC 78-74249
ISBN 978-1-56792-554-8
ISBN 978-1-56792-494-7 (ebook)
ISBN 978-1-56792-710-8 (revised edition)

THIRTEENTH PRINTING. 2021
Printed in Canada

To the memory of
Wesley and Kate Wells

CONTENTS

A man was cleaning the attic of an old house in New England and he found a box which was full of tiny pieces of string. On the lid of the box there was an inscription in an old hand: "String too short to be saved."

ONE

THE WILD HEIFERS

M Y GRANDFATHER always put his heifers out to pasture in the spring, on a lot about five miles from the house, and visited them once a week to salt them, grain them, and see that they had water. In the summer of 1943, when I was fourteen, the heifers broke out of their pasture in early June, and my grandfather had been unable to approach them with the bags of salt and grain. We heard about them as they appeared all over the country. My grandfather had hoped that some piece of luck would box them up again, that they would wander into a barn one night and poke their heads into some empty stalls, or even blunder back to their own pasture. Heifers had gone wild before, and he wasn't going to let it worry him.

In September the hay was in and the talk I overheard at Henry Powers' post office and store was of harvest and frost. Now it was the week I would leave the farm, to go back to Connecticut and to school. I hated school, and I already began to be homesick for the summer. We lingered at night in the kitchen while I had a glass of milk and my grandfather a bowl of bread and milk and my grandmother a glass of Moxie before going to bed. The kitchen floor was bare and gray, unpainted and unwaxed, but scrubbed until it looked as soft as balsa wood. I stared at it and listened to the liquid sounds we made. My grandfather told a story that Thursday night about some young cattle of John Peabody's that had stayed out all winter. People had seen them in February with icicles hanging from their nostrils and ice shining from their leather sides, but blowing forth in white steam a proof of life. In April when the snow melted John had to shoot

1

them like deer and use the carcasses for meat and shoes. I knew that the next day we would hike to catch our heifers.

After the morning chores we ate lunch at eleven-thirty and started down the macadam toward Jacob Buck's woodlot, where we had heard the heifers reported three days earlier. It was a twomile walk. I tried to remember not to let my legs pump out too fast, since my grandfather sometimes felt a pain in his side when he was winded. Few cars were on the road that summer, compared to the numbers in years before or since, but that noon a convoy of army trucks loaded with soldiers kept us single file on the edge of the ditch. We stayed close, his legs nearly cutting under mine, so that we could talk.

The day had begun warm, end-of-summer, dry with the energy of September, but now the sky to the west had turned gray. The wind shifted, and I turned to look at my grandfather. He nodded. "I fear it will rain on us before we're done," he said. "I reckon we can stand a little wet, if we're leading the heifers home." I knew what would come next. Rain or the lost heifers would bring to his mind and his tongue some anecdote of the past and he would recount it to me. I don't remember what it was, this time. His memory was great, and his curiosity, and the two kept his voice active with stories out of his youth and manhood. We could have walked ten years without breaking the links of anecdote or repeating a single one. When we were haying I would try to pitch on while he loaded, so that his breath could be saved for talk. At night in the tie-up while he was milking, he would tell stories or recite long poems he had memorized years before to speak as pieces at the Lyceum. The stories were various and anything might recall them. Walking along the road, he might point out a cellar hole, or distinguish for me in the distance a particular hill, covered with maple now, which his father had cultivated; the recognition would start him on the track of a character or an event. Usually his stories were funny, but they were not jokes. He never began, "There was a man who ..." but "Once Herbert Perkins ..."

I remember once we were talking about droughts, and I

heard the snorting laugh which told me that he remembered a story. "Did I ever tell you," he said, "what Ben Bluitt said to the Reverend Everrill over in Wilmot Flat?" I shook my head and waited. "Old Ben never amounted to much. When I knew him he was back from the war twenty years. He did odd jobs and took care of his granddaughter. She ran away with the lumber man who lost his nose in the sawmill, or so he said, you remember. He drank quite a bit then, beer and rum, but my, he was quick with an answer. I must have told you a hundred things he said. Well, one summer there was a terrible drought over to Wilmot Flat, here too, and Ben was fixing some shingles that had come loose on the church. It was going to take him two weeks, a slow worker, and he would get four dollars and a quarter from the Reverend Everrill, but there wasn't probably much else for Ben to be doing just then. Now the Reverend Everrill was a good man, good, but not a working preacher like Elder Morrill and a womanish kind of fellow, too. He wouldn't work six days in the field and then preach four hours a Sunday. Men didn't take to him much. They said he was happiest when the King's Daughters asked him to come to a circle. He walked past Ben five or six times a day, walking to and from the parsonage with Ben squatting on the roof of the church in the sun, and every time he'd pass by he'd say, 'My' "—and here my grandfather's voice became a falsetto—" 'Mr. Bluitt, have you ever seen such a dry time?' Old Ben never said anything at all, except one afternoon when the old preacher came by one time too many. He said up at Ben, 'My, Mr. Bluitt, have you ever seen such a dry time?' and Ben looked down at him and said, 'Never in my life' "—my grandfather's voice was low and solemn—" 'Reverend Everrill. This morning we had to soak the old sow before she'd hold swill.' "Grandfather's voice expired in laughter, and I joined him. "And he never did ask old Ben any more about the dry time," he said.

We walked past the sap house and the fallen-in shop, old outbuildings from the more prosperous past; part of a lathe stood up among the clutter of broken tools and rotten wood.

Further on we passed the washed-out bottom of New Canada Road, which trailed up Ragged Mountain to a community of cellar holes and stone doorsteps. Three hundred yards further was the red cottage, whose shingles were prying loose from the ravages of ivy, in which my great-uncle, the minister Luther Keneston, had lived until his death the year before. Ahead of us on the right we saw the tumbling house and barn of Ned Masters, my grandfather's old friend. On the other side of the road, half a mile further, we could see the white clapboard of Jacob Buck's house, but we would come to the woodlot before we had walked so far.

I saw a figure moving toward us in the distance, walking in the dirt on the other side of the road. There were no tramps on the road in 1943, and though I sometimes played at imagining that the ditches were full of German prisoners escaped from Canada, this time I knew who it was. Jacob Buck's son was the only boy of my age within two miles, and between us had grown a fiction of friendship from our births, when our mothers had started it. Robert was perfectly all right by me, and we never fought, but I liked books and the country, and he liked automobiles and the city. We hadn't much to say to each other. I knew that on an afternoon when he didn't farm for his father, who was the R.F.D. man and only a part-time farmer, he would often walk four miles to the nearest garage to watch the mechanic work on a car. I guessed that this afternoon was one of his vacations. School would start soon for him, too. My grandfather recognized him when he drew nearer, and said to me, "Why, here's Robert. Isn't it nice that you can say a word to him?" for he acquiesced in the fiction.

"Hi," I said.

"Hi," said Robert.

"We're out to catch the heifers," I said.

"Need any help?" he said and looked uneasy.

"No, Robert," said my grandfather. "You go on down to McLeod's. We're enough to handle it."

"What have you been doing lately?" I said.

"Haying," said Robert.

He said no more and I could think of nothing at all to say. Then Robert thought of a day two years past when the Boley twins had still lived in South Danbury and Billy Cutler had come down from Potter Place and the five of us had batted a ball in a pasture one hot afternoon. "It's too bad the Boleys moved away," he said, "or we could play some more baseball."

"I wish we could too," I said. "Maybe sometime we can play catch anyway."

"Yes," said my grandfather, "you come up, Robert, and you boys can play. Tomorrow maybe."

"I will," said Robert, and he shifted his feet toward McLeod's Garage. "I guess I'll get on."

"Goodbye," we said. We walked on until we came to the woodlot. "It's too bad," my grandfather said, "that you and Robert don't see more of each other."

"Yes," I said.

Then we struck off the blacktop on to a lumber road, barely visible fifteen years after the cutting, which led into a lot of good, new pine. Needles had filled the ruts, and small pines and an occasional miniature maple grew in the old track. I wondered where to start looking, and watched my grandfather to see what he did. "We're trackers today," he said. "Where would you go if you wanted to pick up tracks?"

I always tried to please him by knowing something I couldn't have picked up in Hamden, Connecticut. "Water," I said. "They'd go for water."

He took off his cap and then brushed gnats away from his neck with it. "That's right. There's usually only the one creek, but I wouldn't swear there wasn't a dozen now, with all this plaguey damp."

After a hundred yards we came into a large oval clearing. I couldn't imagine why the pine had chosen not to grow there; the blank was like a birthmark. Underfoot were long yellow strands of hay and unmoved fieldstones. "It's over there," he said, "down the slope."

I looked, and at the edge of the clearing, just before the pines began again, the grass showed a bright green. I moved toward it and saw a steep bank with pine growing out of it and the big creek at the bottom. "Shall we go down?" I said.

"Go to," he said. The bank was deep with needles. I slipped down in a hurry, blocking my way by grabbing at branches and stopping my feet on stumps. He followed more slowly. When he reached me, he said, "Talk low. They'll run when they hear us." A big bird clambered up across the creek and I jumped as if a heifer had landed on my back. My grandfather laughed quietly. Trees along the edges were growing out of the water; The creek was full and moving fast in the middle. The old man shook his head. "I thought that one of us could cross over and look for fresh tracks across the way, but that'll be hard. Suppose you climb up to the rim and walk along the edge, while I look around down here. You know a cow's mark from a deer's, don't you?" I thought I did, and started to pull myself up the wall of needles, but a hiss from my grandfather brought me back. "Come here," he whispered. He was pointing at the ground. I looked down and saw the heifers' tracks. "They've been here all right." He was grinning. "We'll find them, though I don't believe this is today's print."

I dug back into the bank, hands and feet tugging at the matting. In a moment or two I made it to the top, out of breath both with the climbing and with the excitement of chasing two young cows. The air was chilly now, chillier than it had been. Wind turned up the wrong sides of the few gray-birch leaves. I stumbled on hidden stones. Here and there the quick purple of a thistle showed against the sparse grass, both soon to die under the wet weight of the snow. On the far side the pine was black; bald and slim for many feet, but dark between the trees, and then high up the detonation of needled branches; at their roots, like blankets over cold ankles, the bright density of ferns.

I walked slowly at the edge of the clearing, for I knew that my grandfather would make a slow journey of it along the creek. At my feet, the tangle of weeds and fieldstones had slowed me down, and I looked at the ground to avoid the frequent holes which some creature had been digging. I wondered what my grandfather would tell me when I asked him what had mined the clearing. Then the brown, furry shape of a woodchuck blurred across my path. It moved so swiftly that it was down a hole before I could turn my head to follow it. When I did turn, I was looking toward the pine on the other side of the clearing again, and I saw what was so unexpected that for a moment I did not react. A young pine sent out a low branch, and under it—boxed by its green line and the green of the ferns underneath—were the heads of two heifers.

We three stood and stared with a kind of intimacy. When I began to think again, it was of how I could call to my grandfather without upsetting the heifers. I moved backward, slowly, trying to move only from the knees down. They shifted. I turned and ran. I stumbled a short way down the bank and came up against a tree. I heard a great thrashing and crashing back above. "Gramp!" I shouted, "they're up here!" I pulled myself quickly up to the clearing again. The frame had emptied and I could hear the bustle of the big heifers in the pines. In a minute I heard a smaller noise behind and my grandfather was striding up to me. He was panting, which bothered me, but we crossed the clearing toward the low pine, and we walked fast. Deep scuffs in the needles showed where the animals had swung around to gallop away. We didn't need to track them. We could follow by sound as they floundered ahead of us, knocking against the low, dead branches. My grandfather and I did not speak. After a hundred yards the noise ahead grew less frantic. The heifers had slowed down.

As far as I could tell, we were walking parallel to the road, back in the direction from which we had come. Since we didn't try to drive the heifers this way or that, it must have been the way my grandfather wanted them to travel. We walked as much as five minutes without speaking, both to save my grandfather's breath and to avoid frightening the animals ahead of us. It was hard, slow walking, although the trail was broken for us. I scratched my face and hands. We crossed two old lumber roads, but we found no sort of path that went in our direction.

The air that we walked in was growing heavier with damp, and it made the sweat run off my face. "We'll catch them," I finally heard beside me, "if the rain doesn't catch us first." After a pause he said, "In a few rods you cut down to the road and run till you come to Luther's old sheep pasture, and open the gate that leads from here, fifty yards in from the road. I'll drive them, and that's where they're heading."

"How'll we tie them?" I asked.

He shook his head and looked through the black needles to the black sky. "It's aggravating," he said, "to have it a thunderstorm." If my grandfather feared one thing it was an electrical storm. He didn't fear it stupidly, head under covers, but as a farmer who has watched barns burn to the ground. Ahead of us I glimpsed a piece of black-and-white hide. "You can cut through to the road by the path up here," my grandfather said.

Then I heard a rumble and another, as if a car with a trailer had crossed a loosely laid wooden bridge. Around my ears and above my head I heard the soft sounds of water in the needles. "It's here," I said. The dark momentarily lightened around us, and I started to count, but before I reached two the hard smack of the thunder was on us and the rain was coming hard. When the thunder stopped I heard a clumsy noise through the rain, and it took me a moment to remember and to realize that the heifers were frightened by the noise and had begun to run again.

My grandfather was shaking his head. The corners of his mouth were tight. "If only it weren't an electrical storm," he said. "We might as well turn left here, anyway," he said. "Ned Masters' barn's right across here." The pines were decent protection from the rain and I didn't like to leave them for a dash across the macadam, but everyone knew that a pine forest was not the place to wait out a thunderstorm.

I was second in file now, and the pace was fast. We jumped across a ditch at the wood's edge onto the macadam. I lifted my head up into the rain to look for cars. The army convoy had spent itself. "Run," said my grandfather, and I did, but I was sopped to the skin by the time I got to the barn. I stood and panted on the dirt floor, watching him walk stoutly in the drenching wind toward me.

We stood in the door and watched the rain which was solid between us and the old house. One end of the barn, the old tie-up, had tumbled in, and the roof leaked around us, but fresh millet lay at our feet, and the signs of a live cow lay in the horse stall behind us. The house looked ready to fall. I had always stared at it on the way to church or the South Danbury store. The chimney curved like the chimney of a very wicked witch, and grass grew out of the roof around its base. The roof sagged and buckled in various depressions. The clapboards were weathered gray, as if they had never known paint. The doors hung loose on broken hinges, the window panes were half newspaper, and the newspaper was yellow and torn. In front of the house, the side we couldn't see from where we stood, rose an elm which looked as old as the house, and as ready to die. Dead branches and gray bark covered the black roof. Still, you could tell by the carving over the front door that it had been built as an elegant farmhouse.

"Ned's had a hard life," said my grandfather. "He's had a lot of trouble with women, wives and daughters both."

"You knew each other when you were boys, didn't you?" I said, fishing for stories.

"He's the one. Ned Masters. I must have played a hundred games of base-ball with him." He always pronounced it base-ball. "Ned was a tolerable bragger, though he did have a fast way of pitching. One Saturday I was playing for Wilmot, catch, and he was playing for South Danbury. There was a man on third base and one out in the ninth inning and we lacked one run of tying them. I hadn't hit the ball all day and when I came up their catcher shouted out to Ned, 'Here's a bounce-'em-out!' and I got riled. Ned threw a mighty fast one and I gritted my teeth at it and swung. We used to turn our old bats ourselves, on a lathe we'd drive with a pedal, like the one where the shop used to be;

ash they were. Well, the ball went over the fielders into some standing hay and I crossed home base before they ever caught up to it, and I don't believe they ever did find it until Robbie Peters was raking after there for his daddy a couple of weeks later. Oh, my, Ned was mad, to lose the game, mad at the catcher for getting me all riled more than anything. Ned looks very old now and he hasn't been very healthy. I would never be surprised to hear that Ned was dead, though it's a hard thing to say."

The rain seemed to come as consistently as ever, but the intervals between lightning and thunder were becoming greater. "Will we go back after the heifers when the rain stops?" I asked.

He shook his head. "If we had hip boots up to the tops of our heads, we might try it, I reckon. Walking in the young stuff and the ferns we'd be wet to the skin all the time, and your grandmother would be provoked. No, we'll have to put it off again. The Ordman boys can help me catch the wild things, though I'd get more use out of you. You and I will have to turn the millet tomorrow, and get it in, and it will be the end of our summer."

For all I knew, I thought, it could be the end of more than that. I felt very conscious, that September, that my grandparents had another winter to live through before I could return to them. The idea of their mortality was never far from the surface of my day, for a flush or a sigh or a hand pressed to a heart brought death to me, as if I had heard someone say the word. It was a pack on my back, and I would feel the sharp, physical pain of their approach to dying, something becoming nothing—or was it my own approach to bereavement that made my side ache?

Across the wet yard and through one of the remaining panes of glass, I saw a movement and then an ancient face. It had long drooping yellow moustaches, and low folds of skin slanted darkly under the eyes, their line like the line of the moustache, making a pattern on the face like two inverted v's. The old man looked out for perhaps fifteen seconds, without expression, like the heifers stiff with curiosity at the edge of the clearing. Then he pulled back out of sight and I thought to speak. "A man was at the window," I said, "an old man."

My grandfather nodded. "If Ned's eyes don't fail him, he'll be after us to visit with him. I don't rightly like to, dripping like this, and Katie will be anxious because of the storm. Yet we couldn't say no." It took the old man three or four minutes, while the rain declined to a steady ordinary density, to hobble around to the shed door and open it. He stood in it, in a white shirt without a collar—and a Sunday shirt on a weekday was poverty—bent forward from the waist in the black doorway. He gestured once for us to cross over to him, and then backed into the interior. Grandfather started across in the rain and I followed him. Inside, I saw on the wall of the shed the rusty barrel of a shotgun without a stock, next to a rack of bamboo fishing rods which were mostly split. My grandfather led me to the door of the kitchen, knocked, and pushed it open.

The smell of food had begun in the shed and was thick in the kitchen. Ned Masters sat in a rocker next to the black flat-top of a huge kitchen stove in which some coals at least were still burning. When we came in he took a quartered stick of green birch from the woodbox at one side of him and dropped it into the stove on his other side. "Sit down, Wesley," he said. Grandfather said that I was Lucy's boy, and Ned nodded at me. There was only one free chair and my grandfather sat in it. I leaned back against the set-tubs covered with worn oilcloth. Against another wall stood a kitchen table with a mail-order catalogue on it marked "Summer Specials 1937." The floor was uneven, and I could feel it give under my weight when I crossed it. Shreds of paper clung here and there to the walls, some plaster was off the ceiling, and a bucket was catching drips from a leak near the shed door.

"You never met Mother," Ned said to my grandfather. "We been married two years." The door next to the kitchen table opened (I could see a wicker sofa in the further room) and a tiny woman shuffled in. My grandfather stood and shook her hand. When I took it, it was so fragile that I barely returned the pressure it gave me. Ned had been saying, "Mother, this is Wesley Wells and this is his oldest daughter's boy." Her answer was to nod, and she made no kind of noise all the time we were there except for the ceaseless shuffle of her slippers. Her feet in them were bare and the skin looked sore. Now she scurried to the stove and found a kettle, which she filled at the kitchen pump and returned to the stove. "Mother is afraid of the lightning," said Ned. "She just took her head out from under the covers after I saw you." The old man laughed slowly. "She's a good woman," he said, "and better than most."

"You've had a hard time, Ned," said Grandfather.

"Reckon I have. Spent six weeks in the hospital in the spring, did you know?"

"I saw you there, Ned, remember, in May?"

"Yes, guess I do, Wesley. Not what I used to be."

I was watching the cat that had slunk in from the parlor. It was the thinnest cat I ever saw, and its hair was falling off in patches. It took a close look at an empty plate on the floor and patrolled the baseboards as if for mice. I heard my grandfather say, "I was just telling the boy about some of our base-ball."

"I remember those days better than last week. Remember I could handle you."

"Not every time, Ned."

Ned laughed and then stopped and said, "Those were the best days, I think, now I look back. Maybe I'm just an old fool. We're not what we used to be."

My grandfather looked over at me, where I leaned against the settubs and watched the cat. He loved to reminisce, but he could never bear the avowal of failure or despair. It was as if he feared complaint of it more than the failure itself, I thought. He always seemed adequate to his own poverty and bad luck, and he never denied a fact in his life. A time I remember really seeing him in depression was over someone else. Once when my father and mother were at the farm with me, we all took a long drive to let my grandfather visit a cousin he had not seen for forty years— since he left town to enlist for the Spanish-American War, from which he had returned to another part of New Hampshire. We heard in detail on the drive over about the cousin's skill as a wrestler, his quick tongue, and his good humor. The fat old man who met us was petulant, womanish, and bitter. He complained of the size of his pension, his wife who was an invalid, of King Franklin the First, and the younger generation. It was during the depression and my grandfather was a New Hampshire Democrat, and kept newspaper pictures of the President pinned on the dining-room wall at the farm. Before we left, the cousin tried to sell my father some insurance, wheedling and grinning like a caricature of the salesman. On the long, cold drive home, my grandfather huddled in a corner of the back seat and no one spoke. When we were back inside the house again he said that maybe the war had cracked his old friend.

Now he only said, "It's the way it has to be, I guess. We're not young men."

"The house is falling in. I know it. People don't think I know it but I do. When my daddy died, the house was white. It has been a hard time, all of it. You remember this house before the tree, Wesley. Tell the boy how it used to be. None of them care."

"The house will stand, Ned." (After Ned died—it was the winter that followed—and Mother went into the Home, people from Boston bought it for taxes and after the war they rebuilt it and they and their children go there now in the summers and talk as if they were born there.) "You have the pension now, and they look after you when you're sick."

"It's getting old, Wesley. You know what it is." Grandfather didn't answer, but I could see that he was moved. For a moment I thought that he was avoiding it because he didn't want to admit it, but as his eyes looked over at me out of his old face I suddenly understood that it was me he didn't want to know. I—who couldn't, in my morbidity and maybe self-pity, look at him without the temptation to weep over his death, to mourn him while he was still alive—I wasn't to understand. Yet what I wasn't to know was not age or the death in him, I realized next, but his sense of it or fear of it, and its presence in everything he told me, the long anthology of his stories recounted as if to a second memory. He was giving his life to me, handing me a baton in a race, and I took his anecdotes as a loving entertainment, when all of them, even the silliest, were matters of life and death.

Later we turned onto the macadam toward home. The air was still heavy, but it felt clean and autumnal. It was beginning to be my favorite season and up in the hills I could see the patches of red which foreshadowed the colors of later in the month. The low red sun picked them out; against the diverse green, the warning red. They were blight or spotty frost but I took them as a signal of what was coming, and they were more dear to me than the vital green. Looking at them made me happy, and I thought no other thoughts. I was whistling and walked faster to my tune than I should have. When I noticed that my grandfather was breathing hard, I slowed down. "Sorry," I said.

My grandfather recovered his breath. "Mine eyes have seen the glory of the coming of the Lord," he said with the emphases of old-fashioned oratory. "It was a march and you marched to it like a fine soldier." I knew he was thinking of the war. Perhaps I would fight in it and perhaps I would be killed. His father had told him stories of Vicksburg, and the one war was all wars for him. Out of a long silence he said, "He's had a hard life, it's true. The first wife was good but she died and Ned took to drink. Then he married a bad woman who ran off with a boy twenty years younger than she was. Then Ned's daughter when she was fifteen got in trouble and Ned tried to shoot the drummer who did it and they put him in jail for a bit, till he calmed down. A couple of years ago Ned married the woman who was there this afternoon. I've met her before but Ned doesn't remember. I don't believe she's very smart but she's a good woman. Last winter Ned went into the hospital at Franklin and now they've got a glass tube in him someplace."

Two days later I left, and in another week I was back at school. In November I had a long, careful letter from my grandfather in which he told how they had captured the heifers. Twice he had tried to catch them with the help of the Ordman boys, but they hadn't been able to drive them properly. Then he had heard about a man twenty miles north who trained bulldogs to catch cattle. They had tracked the heifers in a light snow. The little dogs bit into the flesh between the nostrils, and when the scared heifers tried to whip them loose, nearly breaking their own necks, the dogs hung on and bit harder. Finally the exhausted heifers hung their heads low while my grandfather slipped halters around their necks to lead them back to the barn.

TWO

THE GALLERY

M Y GRANDFATHER's father was John Wells, a blacksmith who lived on a hill three miles from the farm of my summers. My grandfather was the sixth of nine children. He never intended to take up his father's profession, and when he was old enough he came down into the valley where the villages were strung like beads along the railway. First he took a job in the hame shop, a wooden factory building whose windowless, blackened frame I saw in my early childhood, before the weight of a winter's snow collapsed it into kindling. The fast saws which cut the wood for the hames were driven by water power, and the air was heavy with wooden dust. After two years he coughed badly every night, and knew that he had to look for other work.

He quit to take a job in a grocery store in Potter Place, and later worked behind a counter in West Andover. He liked the jobs because he could talk with people all day, while he measured the bulk flour, sugar, candy, nails, rope, molasses, and cloth. At night he sat with the drummers in the lobby of the Potter Place Inn. He told me about those evenings, and I have an image of him as he was then: young and tall, with a full head of hair, he sits and listens and smiles but rarely speaks; he has a cigar in his hand which keeps going out, and which he lights with large wooden matches.

Soon he would give up cigars, and never smoke again. Those evening cigars were almost his only experience of corruption. It was at this time, too, that he took his trip to Boston. With his brother Bill and two friends he rode the cindery train to the city and watched Ted Lewis pitch for Boston and beat the New York Highlanders. I have heard the game in detail, fifty years after it was played. On the way back to the train, in a saloon near the new North Union Station, my grandfather drank part of a glass of beer. He didn't like it, and he never drank again. He hadn't signed the Temperance Pledge when he was twelve, like my grandmother, but his brother Bill took to drink in later years, and he learned to hate alcohol.

He had known my grandmother from Sunday School. Though he went to church every Sunday, he refused to become a church member (until he was seventy, and my grandmother finally persuaded him) because he said he was not good enough. My grandmother was daughter of a big farmer, and higher on the social scale than the son of a back-country blacksmith. I think he was always conscious that he had married above himself. My grandmother had planned to be a missionary doctor, and when she was a senior at her high school was preparing to enter the Woman's Medical College of Baltimore. Then her mother was suddenly ill, and the local doctor called the pains in her stomach acute indigestion; she felt better suddenly, and just as suddenly she fell into a coma and died. A later doctor shook his head and said, "Appendicitis, rupture, peritonitis." My grandmother's elder sisters were married. She could do nothing but abandon her dreams of Africa, and stay home to keep house for her father.

Benjamin Keneston's family lived first in a farmhouse off New Canada Road, but twenty years later, and just before the birth of the last child, who was my grandmother, Benjamin bought the farmhouse I knew. He kept its Greek-revival front intact, and added rooms and sheds in the back; inside, he bricked up the fireplaces and replaced the small panes of glass with big ones. It was to this farm that my grandfather moved when he married, and as son-in-law took the place of the son who was not a farmer. My grandfather himself had not intended to farm, but it came naturally enough to him. Old Benjamin lived with them, and even accompanied the bride and groom on their honeymoon. Though my grandfather began soon enough to do most of the work, Benjamin made the decisions for twelve years, until he died at eightyseven in 1914.

First my mother, then Aunt Caroline and Aunt Nan were born, and the three girls went to Bates College in Lewiston, Maine, on the sale of timber from woodlots. My mother met my father there. Though Caroline and Nan married, I was the only grandchild of Kate and Wesley Wells.

And so I spent my summers on the farm, by choice and through love of the people and the place. My mother and father would visit for a week or two, but I stayed alone with my grandparents most of the warm vacation months between school and school. The farmhouse was white, and its shutters were the usual deep green of New England. The paint was good, even in the poorest times. My grandmother's flowers showed themselves against the white clapboard, especially in her favorite round bed in front of the kitchen windows. She could look at them while she cooked, or washed workclothes at the set-tubs.

Across the yard, between the cow barn and· the road, was a bigger garden which was bright with phlox and zinnias and petunias. Beyond was a pasture where the color changed as the wild flowers moved through the seasons: yellow and orange paint brushes at first, then wild blue lupines and white Queen Anne's lace, and finally the goldenrod of August. Mount Kearsarge loomed over the pasture in the blue distance, shaped like a cone with a flattened point on top. We sat on the porch and looked at garden, field, and mountain.

The sitting room was crowded with flowers too. Pots stood in a row beside the windows which gave on the porch. Many of them had lost their proper names for familiar ones, like The Connecticut Plant, which derived from the town where Uncle Luther had preached; and The Mother Plant, a huge old-fashioned begonia which had been my great-grandmother's favorite, and whose hairy pointed leaves leaned toward the light. Next to it an old heavy Christmas cactus grew beside the rooted cuttings of geraniums.

In the sitting room, with its low figured metal ceiling, were a piano and a bookcase, a sofa, a radio, and three big chairs. My grandfather always sat in the Morris chair while he read in the evening, and I, if I was not pacing up and down, read in one of the easy chairs. The sitting room was cool in the summer, for the porch shaded the one row of windows. The low winter sunlight entered freely through the same windows, and an iron stove in the far comer burned cordwood to keep the room warm.

Here and in the unused parlor my grandmother kept a gallery of pictures of the family. Most of the faces belonged to men and women who had died before I was born, but I memorized their names, and my grandfather's stories which gave life to the names. From the top of the piano and the bookcase, the rows of faces seemed to regard me as their survivor. Daguerreotypes, tinted photographs, yearbook groups in cap and gown, blurred Brownie snapshots, field-hockey teams, wedding portraits, silhouettes, pictures taken when the subject knew he was dying, Automatic TakUr-Own-Pix, and the crayon drawings you can commission at county fairs for a dollar. There was even the old framed photograph of a favorite cat, a little out of focus and indistinguishable from any other cat. The whole air of the conglomerate past spoke out to me, even the school pictures of my mother and my aunts, which perpetuated a dead girlishness among old hair-dos. To be without a history is like being forgotten. My grandfather did not know the maiden names of either of his grandmothers. I thought that to be forgotten must be the worst fate of all.

THREE

A HUNDRED THOUSAND
STRAIGHTENED NAILS

I F I grew morbid from company with the dead, it was not my grandfather's fault. He was interested only in lively stories about them, and he lived so completely in the dramatic scenes of his memory that everything was continually present to him. My grandmother was occasionally elegiac, but not enough to influence me. When I was nine I saw my Great-Aunt Nannie, blind and insane, dying for one long summer on a cot in the parlor, yet my own lamentation for the dead and the past had begun even earlier. Many of my grandfather's lively stories were symptoms, to me and not to him, of the decay of New Hampshire; a story might include a meadow where the farm boys had played baseball, or a wood through which a railroad had once run.

I found myself, too, taking some of the characters in his stories at a value different from his. So many of them lived a half-life, a life of casual waste. He often talked about Washington Woodward. I knew Washington well, yet my image of him was a mixture of what I had observed and what my grandfather had told me. The whole farm was composed of things which Washington had made or at least repaired, so there was no end of devices to remind my grandfather of a story about him. Most of them were funny, for Washington was eccentric, yet after I had finished laughing, even perhaps when I lay in bed at night and thought over what had happened in the day, the final effect of the stories was not comic. I turned Washington into a sign of the dying place. I loved him, and I could feel his affection for me. Yet when I thought of the disease that afflicted New Hampshire, I knew that my grandfather's face was the exception to disease. The face of sickness was the mouth and moving beard, the ingenious futility of Washington Woodward.

It was a paradox, for he hated corruption and spied it everywhere like a prophet. Yet unlike a prophet he retired from corruption to the hills, meditated it, and never returned to denounce it. He bought a few acres high up New Canada Road, on Ragged, in 1895. He lived there alone, with few forays into the world, for more than fifty years until he died.

I have seen pictures of him, in the farmhouse gallery, taken when he was a young man. He was short and muscular of body, handsome and stem, with a full black moustache over a down-curved mouth. I remember him only as old, for even in my first memories he must have been nearly seventy. The image I retained had him bent nearly double from the waist, with quick bright eyes and his mouth jiggling his beard in an incessant monotone.

When he was young, my grandfather told me, he was already the misanthrope who would exile himself. He had been the youngest of eleven children in a family related to my grandmother. His father, everyone admits, was lazy and mean. Their house burned down, and the children were boarded with various relatives. Washington was only six but already embittered and even surly when he came to live with the Kenestons. My grandmother was a baby. He stayed until he was twelve, and he always looked back to those years as a golden age; my grandmother's family was the great exception to the misanthropic rule. To my grandmother, he was an older brother; when she nursed him during illnesses late in his life, she was remembering someone who had been kind to her, when she was as dependent as he had become.

He would never have left the Keneston house of his own will. When Washington was twelve, his father drove into the farm yard on his broken-down wagon and called for him until he came out of the barn where he had been wandering with little Katie. Washington knew the sort of man his father was, but he knew that sons obeyed fathers. When he had reached the wagon his father told him to lift a hundred-pound sack of grain out onto the ground, and then back into the wagon again. When he did it without straining, his father said, "You're big enough to work. Get packed up. You're coming home."

Washington ran away four years later and set up on his own as a hired hand and an odd-jobber. He was a hard worker and skillful. The best thing about him was his pride in good work. By the time he was twenty-five, he had repaired or built everything but a locomotive. Give him a forge and some scraps of old iron, my grandfather said, and he could make a locomotive too. I knew him to shoe a horse, install plumbing, dig a well, make a gun, build a road, lay a dry stone wall, do the foundation and frame of a house, invent a new kind of trap for beavers, manufacture his own shotgun shells, grind knives, and turn a baseball bat on a lathe. The bat was made out of rock maple which was so heavy that I could barely lift it to my shoulders when he made it for my thirteenth birthday. The problem was that he was incredibly slow. He was not interested in your problem, but in the problems of the job itself. He didn't care if it took him five weeks to shingle an outhouse which plumbing was going to outmode in a year. This was one outhouse that would *stay* shingled, although the shingles might protect only the spiders and the mother cat.

His slowness cost him money, but money did not matter to him. He did not even call it an abomination like drinking, card-playing, smoking, swearing, lipstick, and dancing; he simply did not think of it. He needed no more for supper than bread and milk. Did anyone else? If he didn't care about money, he cared about people sticking to their word; he cared about honor whether it concerned his pay or the hour at which he promised to finish a job. Once a deacon of the church asked Washington to fix the rickety wheels of a carriage. Washington told him it would be four dollars and he spent six full days at the forge strengthening the wheels and adding supports until the axles would have carried five tons of hay, much less the deacon and his thin wife. But the deacon said, when the carriage was delivered, that four dollars was too much, and that three dollars was what the job was worth. Washington refused to take anything, and never sat in his pew again, for if deacons cheated, churches were corrupt. He read his Bible by himself.

During all his years of solitude, he was extraordinarily sociable whenever he saw his family, as if the taciturnity he had assumed with his solitude was unnatural. He stored up, alone in his shack, acres of volubility which the sight of a relative discovered. If I remarked to him that an apple he had given me was a good apple, he might say, "Well, I remember; that apple came from the tree by the woodchuck hole in the northeast corner that leans toward the south; though it don't lean much; down in that patch there; it's from a graft, that branch is, from a big tree, high as a house, on John Wentworth's land; his orchard behind his cow barn beside the sap house; well, the tree, old John Wentworth's been dead twenty years' tree, was always a good one for apples, big and meaty with plenty of juice to them; and one summer about 1919, no, 1920 I guess, I was working up to John's; I was fixing some sap pails had leaks and I shingled the ice-shed, the back of it, where you couldn't see from the road but it was about gone; I'd done the front before and I told him the back would need doing; I was there as much as two months, ten weeks I guess; and it come apple time while I was there, and I helped him picking and he come up here and helped me; and I had my few trees up here, not so many as now, not half so many, as I reckon it, and one time I was mending a water pipe that fed the horse trough, it had come loose, and John didn't have no more solder, so I had to come all the way back to the shop; and as I was going I stopped to look at the tree, the big one, and I thought about asking John if I could splice off a limb as part pay; well, I never did get back that day because I saw a deer in the peas when I got here..." and he would tell how he waited for the deer and shot him, and what he had done with the pelt, and what John Woodward had said to him when he asked for the limb, and how he had spliced it to his own tree, and on and on until, if the body had been strong enough, Washington would have talked out the whole contents of his mind. Scratch him anywhere and you touched his autobiography. Any detail was sufficiently relevant if it kept the tongue moving, and the silence broken. My grandfather's many memories, on the other hand, were separated into stories with just enough irrelevant material of the past to keep them circumstantial; they had form, and you knew when he had come to a stopping point. Washington was a talking machine capable of producing the recall of every sensation, every motive, of a lifetime; and all the objects of his world could serve him like Proust's madeleine.

It was not the past that interested him, but talking. If he had known about contemporary politics, he would have been willing to use it as his pretext for speech, but in the pursuit of independence he had cut himself off from everything but his daily sensations. The talking was the same when he was young and when he was old. When we visited him at his shack, he would invariably trot alongside the car or buggy as we left, jogging a hundred yards further with the story he couldn't end. My mother remembers from her girlhood, and I from twenty-five years later, how my grandparents would go to bed while he was talking, and how he would drone on for hours in the dark. When he was old and sick, he would talk in his chair in the kitchen while they read in the living room. Sometimes he would laugh a little and pause, as he reached a brief resting space in his unfinishable monologue. My grandmother learned to say, "Is that so?" whenever there was a pause. My grandfather swore that she could do it in her sleep.

Washington always wore the same costume in the years I knew him. The only thing which ever differed about his appearance was his beard, for he shaved in the summer and let his hair grow for warmth in the winter. He wore heavy brown overalls, patched and stitched, and a lighter brown work shirt stitched so extensively that the cloth had nearly vanished under the coarse thread; over these he wore a light nondescript work coat and in winter a thick, ancient overcoat with safety pins instead of buttons. He often spent his evenings sewing by the light of a candle until his eyes hurt.

Washington had built his shack on the slope of Ragged Mountain on the western, downward side of New Canada Road, two miles up from U.S. 3 by the road, but half a mile as the crow flies. He had a small pasture for cattle, a hen yard, geese wandering loose, a good orchard of apple trees and other northern fruits, and at various times he kept pigs, goats, ducks, and a dog. His shack was small, and it had grown smaller inside every year. Layers of things saved grew inward from the walls until Washington could barely move inside it. A tiny path among the boxes and animal pelts led from the door to a cross path from iron stove to a Morris chair. Washington slept upright in the chair every night.

If he found a board in a ditch as he walked home from the day's work, and if the board had a bent nail in it, he would hammer the nail out of the board with a rock and take it home. If the board would make kindling or if it was strong enough to build with, he would take it along too. He would straighten the nail with a hammer on the anvil at his lean-to shop, and put it in a box with other nails of the same dimensions. He might have to move a dozen other boxes to find the right one, but he would know where it was. It wasn't that he was a miser, because he cared nothing for the money he saved by collecting used nails. And when he died he did not, like the misers reported in the newspapers, leave a hundred thousand dollars in the back of a mirror; he left a hundred thousand straightened nails. He saved the nails because it was a sin to allow good material to go to waste.

Besides nails, Washington kept a complete line of hardware and parts: clasps, hinges, brackets, braces, hoe handles, ax heads, and spare rungs for ladders. He also saved elk, moose, bear, beaver, fox, and deer pelts. On the wall beside the door were his rifle and shotgun and boxes of shells and cartridges. He was a good shot and a patient hunter. Until he was old he shot a big buck every year and ate nothing but venison until the bones were bare. Once a year, in the early fall, he had my grandmother bake him a woodchuck in her big oven. Only when his legs were so bad that he did not dare to wait out an animal, for fear that he would not be able to move after being still, did the woodchucks and hedgehogs manage to eat his peas and apples, and avenge their ancestors.

He ate one kind of food exclusively until he finished his supply of it. Often it would be nothing but oatmeal for a week. Again he would buy two dozen loaves of stale bread and eat nothing else until the last mouldy crust was gone. I remember him eating his way through a case of corn flakes, and when the woodchucks had eaten his garden, one winter he ate a case of canned peas. It was no principle with him, but simply the easiest thing to do. When he was old and sick, living a winter in the rocking chair in my grandmother's kitchen beside Christopher, the canary, he bought his own food and kept it separately, in a cardboard box beside him. At this time he had a run on graham crackers. He did not eat on any schedule, and sometimes my grandparents would wake up in the middle of the night to hear him gumming a cracker, his false teeth lost in the darkness of a Mason jar.

When he was younger he must have been nearly self-sufficient. For much of each year he would refuse outside jobs from anyone, unless my grandfather particularly needed a mowing machine fixed or a scythe handle made when the store was out of scythe handles. And often he wouldn't take any money from my grandfather, although my grandmother would try to pay him in disguise with shirts and canned vegetables and pies. To pay the taxes on his land he worked a few days a year on the county road gang, repairing the dirt roads that criss-crossed the hills like shoelaces and connected the back farms with the main road in the valley. For clothing he had his gifts, and I know that he once made himself a coat out of fur he had trapped. For food he had all the game he shot, and he kept potatoes and apples and carrots and turnips in a lean-to (the food covered with burlap a foot thick to keep it from freezing) beside his shack, and he canned on his small stove dozens of jars of peas, tomatoes, corn, and wax beans.

When he took an outside job or made a little money by ped-
dling patent medicines like Quaker Oil or Rawleigh's Salve, he
might buy himself a candy bar or five postcards or a pad of paper, or he might give it away. When my mother and her sister
were at college, they sometimes had a letter from Washington
with a nickel carefully wrapped inside. The patent medicines
were before my time, and my grandfather told me about them.
Washington would occasionally fill a large basket with his vials
and jars, cut himself a walking stick, and set out to peddle on
the back roads. He would sleep in barns, barter for his food, and
return after a week with a pocketful of change. A room on the
second floor of the farmhouse was always full of cases marked
in the trade name of a cough syrup or a tonic. Everyone in the
family sniffed up drops of Quaker Oil to stop sneezing, or ate a
few drops on a lump of sugar for coughing.

Washington worked hard at tending his trees and garden and
animals, and when he was through with his chores he invented
more work for himself. He spent considerable time and energy at what I can only call his hobby. He moved big rocks. His
ingenuity, which was always providing him with new, usually
trivial tools (tools which took him four days to make and which
simplified a fifteen-minute job); invented a massive instrument
of three tall pine logs and an arrangement of pulleys. It looked
like the tripod of a camera, but the camera would have been
as big as a Model A. By means of this engine, he was able to
move huge rocks; I don't know how he moved the whole con-
traption after the rock was lifted, though when I was a boy I
must have heard detailed descriptions of a hundred rock-moves.
(I was another who learned to shut the door between his ears
and his brain.) He moved any rock for whose displacement he
could find an excuse: small boulders that obstructed his fields;
rocks near the house whose appearance offended him; rocks beside the road into which a car might sometime, possibly, crash;
rocks, even, in the way of other peoples' cows in other peoples'
pastures. When he was old and couldn't use the machine any
more, it weathered beside the front door of his shack, and when

he died someone took it away for the pine.

It was the cows he was thinking of, not the farmers, when he moved rocks in a pasture. He often insisted that, except for his family and one or two others, humanity was morally inferior to animals. He himself had developed a gorgeous line of cattle, out of a combination of devotion and shrewd trading. It was when I knew him that he had Phoebe, the last beast that he truly loved. Phoebe was a Holstein, a prodigy among milkers and the only cow in the world that thought it was a collie dog. Treated like a house pet from birth, she acted like one with Washington. She came frisking to him when he called her, romped with him, and all but whined when she couldn't follow him into the shack and curl her great bulk at his feet. Washington fed her apples and peas in the pod while he ate stale bread. She slept on the other side of a plank wall from him, so that he could hear any irregularity in her breathing. He washed her every day. When she was old and lame, Washington invented a rig like his rock-mover to help her stand or lie down. He nursed her when she was sick, and he was caressing her when she died.

My grandfather told me about an earlier pet, Old Duke the ox. Washington taught Old Duke to shake hands and roll over. He made a cart and a sled which Old Duke could pull, and it would take him a whole forenoon to drive the two and a half miles from his shack to the farmhouse. The only time Washington ever showed romantic interest in a woman was when a young girl named Esther Dodge helped out at the farm one harvest. Washington paid court by asking Esther, a pretty red-cheeked country girl as my mother remembers her, for a ride behind Old Duke. Esther would only go if the girls, my ten-year-old mother and her younger sister Caroline, could come along, and they giggled all the way.

When Washington was seventy-nine, Anson Buck found him in a coma one morning when he came to deliver a package on his R.F.D. route. Anson carried him into the back seat and drove fourteen miles to the hospital at Franklin, where they operated. When he recovered, he went back to his shack. One day the following December, my grandmother made some mince pies and decided to send one to Wash. She flagged down a young lumberman as he passed by in his blue 1934 Chevrolet and asked him to leave it off on his way up New Canada to work. He was back almost as soon as he left, saying, "He's looney, Old Wash is looney." After Great-Aunt Nannie, no such announcement was liable to surprise my grandmother. She called "Yoo-hoo," to the barn and told my grandfather what had happened. The lumberman drove them to the shack.

They found Washington sitting on the floor of his cabin between his sleeping chair and his cold stove, which my grandfather said hadn't been lit all night. Washington didn't seem to notice that they were there but kept on talking as they had heard him talk before they entered. What he said was incoherent at first, but they could tell that it was about building a road, about white hogs, and about two ladies. He allowed himself to be helped over the thick snow into the Chevrolet and driven back to the house.

Washington told his story for many days, over and over, until my grandparents finally understood its sequence. My grandfather told me all about it the next summer. The night before he was found, Wash said, he took a walk to look at a timber lot of my grandfather's north of his shack. (His legs were so bad that he never walked any further than his well that winter; the timber was three-quarters of a mile away.) When he got there he saw a whole crowd of people working, though it was nearly dark, and they were cutting a big new road. They had bulldozers, which were white, and a big herd of white horses. He walked up to some of the people and tried to talk to them, but they acted as if they couldn't see him, and they were jabbering in a language he couldn't make out, but it wasn't Canuck. He walked away from the crowd and climbed a little rise, and when he looked down on the other side of the rise to a cleared field he saw about a hundred hogs, all pure white. In front of them were the biggest sow and the biggest boar he had ever seen, both pure white, and they were mating. Washington started to walk down the hill and he stubbed his boot on the nose of a horse that was sticking up through the snow. He and the horse fell in the snow, down and down, until the people lifted them up on the huge piece of chicken wire that was underneath the snow. Then two women among the people took him back to his cabin and stayed there all night with him. He watched, all night long, the tips of their hats against the background of starlight from the cracks in the cabin walls. Though he asked them questions, they never answered.

The doctor came and listened to Washington and gave him morphine. When he woke up he seemed fine except that he kept on with his story. My grandfather told him that there was no road going into his timber lot, and Washington was only indignant. After a week he began to ask visitors about the road, and they all told him there wasn't any, and he stopped telling the story. In the spring he paid a boy with a flivver to drive him past the place so that he could see with his own eyes.

He never had delusions again. Perhaps he had left his cabin for water and had fallen in the snow when his legs failed him. Perhaps he had crawled for an hour in pain through all that whiteness back to his shack where he had talked to the boxes all night. By April he was back at his cabin again, and that summer he was eighty years old.

He died in a state nursing home. My grandfather and I went to see him a month before he died, and his cheeks were flushed above the white beard, and his eyes shone while he performed his monologue. He joked with us and showed us the sores on his legs. He displayed me to his nurses and to the silent old men in the room with him. It was a little like all the other times I had met him, yet seeing him ready to die I was all the more impressed by the waste of him—the energy, the ingenuity, the strength to do what he wanted—as he lay frail and bearded in a nightgown provided by the legislature. The waste that he hated, I thought, was through him like blood in his veins. He had saved nails and wasted life. He had lived alone, but if he was a hermit he was neither religious nor philosophical. His fanaticisms, which might have been creative, were as petulant as his break from the church. I felt that he was intelligent, or it would not have mattered, but I had no evidence to support my conviction. His only vision was a delusion of white hogs. He worked hard all his life at being himself, but there were no principles to examine when his life was over. It was as if there had been a moral skeleton which had lacked the flesh of the intellect and the blood of experience. The life which he could recall totally was not worth recalling.

Standing beside him in the nursing home, I saw ahead for one moment into the residue, five years from then, of Washington Woodward's life: the shack has caved in and his straightened nails have rusted into the dirt of Ragged Mountain; though the rocks stay where he moved them, no one knows how they got there; his animals are dead and their descendants have made bad connections; his apple trees produce small and sour fruit; the best-built hayracks rot under rotting sheds; in New Hampshire the frost tumbles the cleverest wall; those who knew him best are dead or dying, and his gestures have assumed the final waste of irrelevance.

FOUR

THE LEFT-FOOTED THIEF

THERE WERE many shacks in Merrimack County which looked like Washington Woodward's. A few belonged to old bachelors, but most of them were hovels in which the nine or ten members of a family would live. These families were the lowlife of the country. I don't think they were an exploited class, for they didn't work until they had to. They were shiftless and inbred and often half-witted. Though a few escaped their destiny, most of them were petty criminals, and spent a part of every year in jail.

One August day, some time in the early forties, my grandfather and I took a hike up New Canada Road to repair some fence in the cow pasture. Near the start of New Canada, we passed an abandoned shack. Half of the roof was sagging in, and the body of a Model T was rusting in the yard in front of it. In back, I could make out a collapsed barn. My grandfather pointed to the shack. "One more winter," he said, "and that'll be down as flat as the barn."

"Godfreys used to live there, didn't they?" I asked. I had heard about the Godfreys in my grandfather's stories, in which they drank and stole and were sent to prison for incest. Most of the people in his stories, and I think most of the people in the society his stories were about, were morally distinct. If you were good you were perfectly good. If you were bad, you overlooked no means of becoming worse. Whoever took a drink finished the jug.

"Yes," he said. "Godfreys lived there. I wonder where the critters are now. Won't know where to look if the barn is missing when we get home."

We climbed in silence for a minute, going uphill. Then he grinned and I knew he had a story. "Did I ever tell you," he said, "how Fred and I caught the sheep-stealer?" His brother Fred had sometimes come over to help out with the chores. I said I didn't remember the story.

"Well," he said, "one day Fred and I set out to salt the sheep. They were in the pasture down by the lake. This was back when your mother was a little girl. When we got there I called the sheep together, ke-day ke-day, and my great prize sheep was gone. I knew she'd been there the day before because I'd stopped to fix the fence on the way back from haying in the Peasely meadow.

"I knew it wasn't a dog because the rest of the sheep were calm and easy. It could have been an accident or it could have been Godfreys, Turpinses, Harrises, or Freedoms. They were the families that did everything bad in Wilmot and West Andover. Fred and I walked along the fence and looked for a break. When we got to the end of the pasture on the road side, Fred looked hard at the fieldstones which were piled at the corner of the fence. 'Somebody's kicked these stones a bit, Wesley,' he said. 'Five years since Wash laid them for you.' He moved one of the stones that was knocked loose and there was the live grass under it. 'Just happened, too.'

"Then I saw a strand of wool on a branch which I'd put across the top of the stones. 'Look at this,' I said. 'I reckon we found something, and I don't reckon the creature jumped.' We both looked in the dirt of the road, but it was hard and we couldn't see any tracks in it. Fred sat the stones back in the wall and climbed over it.

" 'Come here, Wesley,' Fred said to me. I climbed over too and looked at a whole passel of footprints, where the shade of the wall and a little bush had kept the grass from growing. There were prints of work boots clear as day among all the hoofprints. 'Early this morning I reckon,' said Fred. 'It rained some up here last night.' We snooped around a bit. 'Reckon there was just one of them,' said Fred. He was a regular detective. 'He boosted and drove your old sheep over here and then drove her where he wanted. In the ditch I reckon, so we couldn't pick up the track.'

" 'I reckon we can try,' I said to him. I wasn't going to give up.

" 'Which way?' he said.

'Let's go back this way first,' I said. Unless they were smart, which wasn't very likely, I knew they'd head for home. And nobody lived up that way who'd steal a sheep. 'Can you tell anything from the boot?' I asked Fred.

'Nope,' said Fred. 'It looks like any old work boot to me.' We crossed the fence and started to walk down the road, looking in the ditch and the road both. Then Fred said, 'I keep thinking there *was* something peculiar about those boot prints.' He looked at the road again, but then he turned around and jogged back toward the comer of the wall. 'Wesley,' he yelled back, 'they're all left-footed!' "

My grandfather paused and looked over at me to see how I was reacting. I laughed at his dramatic line, and told him to keep on, and that he had me all excited.

"Well," he said, "I looked, and they were, too. We didn't know what to think. We walked down to the main road, and talked about it. We decided it probably wasn't a one-legged thief or a hopping thief. 'Well,' said Fred, 'where do you look for a man with two left feet?'

" 'I reckon you look for his brother with two right feet,' I said, and I didn't know how much I said either.

" 'There are some folks around here stupid enough to mix up their boots,' said Fred. 'What do you plan to do, Wesley?'

"I told him to come and have some dinner and that then we'd hitch up and drive down to tell Lester about it. Lester was the one who'd have to take someone to jail. We ate and then we drove Ginger down to Potter Place, where Lester Foster was. I did some thinking on the way. 'It's a Turpin or a Godfrey,' I told Fred. 'It couldn't be a Freedom because all the Freedom boys are in jail. The Harrises got poisoned from drinking some stuff William Henry Harrison Godfrey made and old Doctor Clough told me yesterday that none of them will get out of bed for a week. No, it's a Turpin or a Godfrey.

"Lester listened to us and said we should let him know when we found anything out. When we were through with Lester, Fred wanted to go to the store. When Fred got in sight of the front window, he stopped as still as a shot rabbit. 'Wesley,' he called out to me, 'maybe you'd better come here.' When I looked in the window, I saw what he meant. There were two work boots in the window, both for the right foot."

My grandfather paused again, both for dramatic effect and because he was out of breath. "Don't stop now!" I said.

"All right," he said, "but let's sit down." We found a tree stump and a stone. "Now, where was I? Well, we went inside the store, Albert Wrigley's. I remember we had to wait until Albert finished selling some rope. We took the boots out of the window and took a good look at them. They were a little different in the making, but they were the same size. There was nothing to keep them from being mates of the boots we were looking for. The man left with his rope and Albert came up to us and said, 'What can I do for you, Wesley?' " My grandfather's voice went into his falsetto. He never had liked Albert Wrigley.

" 'Albert,' I said to him, 'who's wearing the mates to those boots in the window?'

"Old Albert jumped nearly out of his skin. 'What you know about them left-foot boots, you Wellses?' he said. I thought he was ready to have us arrested. 'Nothing,' I said, 'except whatever stole them from you stepped into them to steal a sheep from me.'

"Albert was surprised, but I told him all about it. 'Doggone him,' he said. 'It was just yesterday. I stepped into the back room for half a minute once all day. It must have been then. When I noticed was when I was closing up. They was in the window and these was in the back.'

" 'All we have to do,' said Fred, 'is lie down on the grass out here and look at feet until we see two left feet taking a walk together.'

"Albert didn't have a sense of humor much. 'Not even a Harris or a Godfrey could be dumb enough to wear them in town,' he said.

"The three of us sat down on the bench beside the coal stove, which wasn't lighted of course because it was summer. We just sat there without saying anything. Then I had a thought. 'Did you mean anything special when you said a Harris or a Godfrey?' I asked Albert. 'Any reason why you didn't say a Turpin or a Freedom?'

'It couldn't be a Turpin or a Freedom,' said Albert. 'Turpins were all in Danbury yesterday and still are today with their cousins, because Rafe Turpin just got a bounty for the wildcat that dropped dead in his hen yard. All the Freedoms are in jail. You know that. I mean the men are. None of the girls would steal men's work boots. Too selfish.'

'You sure about the Turpins?' I said.

" 'Sure as can be,' he came back. 'Thought about it a lot. Rafe was here yesterday morning for tobacco when they was starting, and after they left for Danbury I took a good look at my stock. The boots was there.'

" 'Then it's a Godfrey!' I said, and I explained why it couldn't be a Harris.

"So that night after everyone was in bed, Fred and I sneaked three miles in the dark to Godfrey's place, same place we just saw. There wasn't any light showing any place. We went into the woods past the house and came around in back of the old barn. It was falling in a bit even then. Fred lit the lantern. The only thing we found was a sap bucket all covered with flies. 'Yep,' I said to Fred, under my breath, 'that's where they caught the blood.' I'd still hoped to find him alive.

" 'Can't hang them on a bucket of blood,' said Fred. 'Where's the pelt?'

" 'They'd hide it,' I said. 'They'd know that much.' So we decided to look outside.

"The moon was up and we stood in the shadows and looked around. The dung heap was next to us, and the yard beyond was where they kept their chickens. 'I'll look in the coop,' said Fred, and he went across the yard. There was some clucking inside, and in a minute he came back shaking his head.

" 'They might be keeping it in the house,' I said.

" 'Stinking thing?' said Fred. 'I suppose they might, being Godfreys. I suppose Lester can get us a warrant if we tell him what we know.'

"But then I looked down and saw a piece of something white sticking out from the bottom of the dung heap next to us. That was what we wanted. That was my pretty sheep's pelt, poor old dear."

My grandfather stood up from his stump and stretched. "My," he said, "I get stiff so soon these days. How was that for being a detective?"

I thought it was pretty easy, when you had only four families to pick your criminal from, but I didn't tell him so. "Did somebody go to jail?" I said.

"Oh, yes," he said. "We came back with Lester after milking the next morning, and we hadn't been there more than five minutes when old William Henry was out there helping us dig out the pelt. He was telling us that Sam, his youngest boy, had done it, and it turned out to be true for once. Lester caught Sam trying to walk south a little later. Lester had a good trotting horse. Sam was limping in those left-footed boots of his."

"Didn't my mother go to school with Sam?"

"Yes, I reckon she did." We were walking again, and we were nearly there. "Not that he went to school much. Lester took him off to jail for the first time that day. He's dead now, Sam. Your mother cried that day, I remember well, because I guess he was a nice boy in his way."

We turned off the road and took down the bars of a gate and stepped into the pasture.

"I want you to remember another good story for the way back," I said. "Remember, it'll be downhill."

FIVE

HAYING, A HORSE,
AND A HIRED MAN

I N MY summers on the farm, I saw only remnants of the flour-ishing low-life of former years. Once when we were riding in the buggy my grandfather pointed out a whole clan squatting vacantly on the dirt in front of an old chicken coop. Their heads turned to watch us, but they showed no expression. "That's what's left of the Turpinses I've told you about," he said.

The only representative of the four families whom I really knew was Anson Freedom, and he was an exception. In fact, he was at least negatively good, for he didn't steal or drink or lech. He was half-witted, but he could work at simple chores, and he was my grandfather's hired man. I knew him first the summer I started haying. In my last summers on the farm, my grandfather and I did the work by ourselves; when I wasn't there my grandfather mowed and raked and brought in the hay by himself. But in my first years of haying there were three of us, and Riley the old horse. I thought of haying as something that my grandfather and Anson and Riley and I did together. Anson's silly grin and Riley's bony rib-cage belong to those hot afternoons in the cut fields, as much as the teasing and story-telling voice of my grandfather.

Anson had been a hired man for my grandfather and Benja-min Keneston thirty years earlier, and he was the clown of my mother's childhood, too. He was the most hideous man I have ever seen. His face, of which the features were cramped to-gether in a squat triangle, was always burned red, but his enor-mous bald head was as white as soap. The skull was wide but not high; it shot back flatly over the four deep lateral wrinkles

39

that crossed above his eyes. His small eyes were surrounded by lines so deep that they looked like make-up. His nose was boneless and flattened between protruding cheekbones. His mouth usually curved upward in an empty-headed grin which created more of the thick, muscular ropes of wrinkles. When he walked he stooped so much he seemed hunchbacked, and his arms swung loosely at his sides.

When my mother was a girl, during the first war, Anson's cousin Lewis induced him to leave the farm for a war job, which could not have been more complicated than sweeping up. Anson did not return until 1939. I heard of it that spring in Connecticut, and I had listened to so many stories about him that it was as if Tom Sawyer had moved into the next block. My grandmother had simply looked out her window, one morning, to see Anson Freedom with twenty years added to him come shuffling up the driveway. At least he seemed to remember that he had left abruptly, for he was afraid to come close enough to knock. He had returned, they learned later, because Lewis had refused to feed him any longer. My grandmother leaned out the door and told him to go to the barn, where Wesley was cleaning the tie-up after milking.

"Hullo," said Anson to my grandfather. My grandfather told me later that he was so surprised he nearly dropped the hoe through the floor to the pile of manure under the barn, but of course he wouldn't let Anson know it. "Why Anson Freedom," he said slowly, "I thought you were dead."

"Now don't yew start plaguin' me!" The pattern that I was to hear so often during our afternoons of haying—the teasing and the half-serious rage which had begun so many years before—had started immediately. One of the subjects on which Anson could be teased was death; I once saw him bend down below the window of a car to avoid seeing a cemetery.

"You come back to work or watch me working?" said my grandfather.

"Kin I work?"

My grandfather thought for a minute. "The truth is I don't

have any money to pay you with, Anson." Milk was fetching
him up to twenty dollars a month, and he had no other regular
cash crop. Eggs paid for the grain he fed the hens, and the chicks
and lambs paid his taxes.

"I got to work."

"A dollar and a half a week, board and room?"

"That's fine." And my grandfather handed Anson the hoe to
finish scraping the manure.

I had been prepared even for the way he talked by my grandfather's imitations of him. It was pathetic to think that he had
changed so little. There is a story I remember about his boast-
ing. He had gone hunting deer with another cousin, and when
he came back he told everyone that he had shot a buck right
through the eye. My grandfather knew that Anson couldn't hit
Ragged Mountain point blank, but he said nothing until one
noon when he had a sudden intuition. My grandfather said,
"Now Anson Freedom, didn't your cousin shoot that buck and
then tell you to go up to it and shoot it through the eye after it
was dead, just so you could tell folks about it? Or maybe because
he'd already shot one himself, and one was all he could shoot on
his license?"

Anson's mouth dropped open wider than ever. "He said he
wouldn't tell nobody, the old fuel!"

In the summers when I knew him, he fished occasionally, but
I never knew him to do anything else but his chores. He seemed
to have only one bodily desire. He was a glutton for candy bars.
Most of his salary, which increased with war prosperity to three
dollars a week, was spent on Milky Ways, Powerhouses, and
Baby Ruths. His closet was littered with empty cases. At night
after supper he would slink off to bed and lie in the dark peeling
off the wrappers and sucking toothlessly at the chocolate bars.

At noon he would come into the sitting room, when my
grandparents listened to the news and weather from a Concord
radio station. One of my summers with him, he became obsessed by a thirty-second advertisement for Peter Paul's Mounds
which an announcer read between the news and the weather.

The rest of us learned not to hear the hired, yum-yumming voice, but Anson believed in the emotion the voice claimed to represent, and his jaws worked sensually as he listened. "Mus' tas' awful good," he said each day.

The problem was that none of the local stores carried Peter Paul's Mounds. Henry Powers, whose little store was post office, gas station, and grocery for West Andover, asked his distributor for a box at Anson's request, but the box never came. Anson began to talk about them at the supper table, during haying, and while he and my grandfather were milking. "Mus' tas' awful good," he would say. One time he found me alone. "Donnie," he said, "you hain't never eaten those Peter Paul's Mounds?" I told him I thought I had, back home in Connecticut, and that I remembered liking them. It was as if I had mentioned to a French teacher who had never left White River Junction, Vermont, that I was a personal friend of Marie Antoinette's.

Once every summer I would spend a day by myself in Concord or Franklin. I would take the Peanut in the morning, leaving at 7:05, and return by the Peanut in the evening, at 7:30. My grandfather would take me down and pick me up in the buggy. In the city, I would wander around the business section, working my way through the news stands, lending libraries, and the book store. I would always end up exhausted in the public library reading the new books. This particular year my big errand was accomplished quickly. The first drug store I came to sold me a box of Peter Paul's Mounds, and I had to carry the box all day.

Anson ran up the stairs with it when I got back and I suspect that he ate all twenty-four bars before the morning chores. He never mentioned them again, but when the ad came over the radio he would look at me and smile with our secret.

THE SUMMER of 1939 I was ten. Anson had returned the April before. I remember the first day I helped in the haying, a hot afternoon in late June. My grandfather was haying on the fields of a widow who lived a mile and a half north on the main road.

She gave her hay to the farmer who would do a neat job, for she hated the look of a field that was left with hay untrimmed around the rocks, and with the scatterings unraked. My grandfather had hay on his own fields, but he liked to help the old lady.

Mornings were for mowing. In the early hours before the hay was dry enough to cut, Anson and my grandfather milked the cows and turned them out to pasture, cooled the milk, fed the hens, picked up the eggs, and set the milk out for the truck. A rainy day was good for repairs to the wagons and machinery, or for splitting wood. A day that threatened rain, or a day when the hay was drying after a rain, might be good for salting the sheep or for paying a visit to the heifers. But if the day was good, Anson would hitch Riley to the mowing machine at nine-thirty or ten, and he could cut a two-acre field by noon. He was a good workman at a job he had done often. My grandfather loved a scythe, and he would trim, coming close to the rocks without ever denting the edge of his blade. In the breast pocket of his work shirt he carried a blue-gray whetstone, and I loved to watch the fast sweeping motion with which he sharpened his blade, leaning the end of the handle in the dirt at his feet. Later, when I was fourteen, he taught me how to use a scythe, and he sharpened an old scythe for me so that I could help him trim.

At noon they usually returned for lunch and a brief rest before the afternoon haying. On the day I was to start my life's haying—doing what my grandfather had done for fifty years—lunch was a special occasion. Since I was not old enough to mow, I would help in the afternoons only. My Aunt Caroline was home that week, and at twelve o'clock we packed a huge laundry basket full of lunch into her car and drove to the widow's field. Near the house itself were a few fruit trees, and under one of them we spread an old quilt. There were a Thermos of coffee and a Thermos of milk, hard-boiled eggs, pork sandwiches, cheese sandwiches, an onion sandwich especially for me, pickles, cake, cookies, and a custard pie.

The brilliant orange and yellow paint brushes grew wild at the edge of the road, and beside the widow's house the lilacs were still blooming. The sky was bright, with only a few clouds, and there was a light breeze from the south. "Good day for hay-ing," said my grandmother.

"I'll *say* it's a good day," said my grandfather.

I noticed that my grandmother had on a new apron, and my grandfather's blue work shirt had the creases of a shirt that has never been washed. He was the most excited of us all. He hummed little songs in his tuneless way, and his eyes were sharp with the occasion. His sweat made the dark shirt darker under his shoulders and in the middle of his chest. His lean arms were burned, and his bald head was pale when he took off the cloth cap he always wore in the sun. He told how he had helped out, a hired boy, for ten cents a day when he had been my age. The farmer had threatened to charge him for drinks of water, out of the horse trough at the barn, when they brought in their loads of hay. "It's a mighty deep well," the farmer had said, "but you look like to drink it dry, Wesley Wells."

When we had eaten the last pickle and had shaken the crumbs from the quilt, Caroline and my grandmother packed the empty basket and the quilt into the Studebaker. My grandmother told me to watch I didn't take too much sun, and to make sure that Gramp was careful when he turned from the field onto the mac-adam on the way home. Then they drove off.

I walked back to the apple tree, where my grandfather was stretched out in the shade, taking a shortened version of his rest after lunch. Anson was sitting cross-legged, chewing on a piece of grass. He smiled at me, and I think he was excited too. I sat down beside him.

In a moment my grandfather leapt to his feet, standing so quickly that it seemed there was no intermediate position be-tween lying down and standing up. "Well, now, you jackrab-bits!" he said. "Anson, you go draw some water for Riley. Don-nie, you come with me and we'll hitch Riley up to the rake." We strode off to the other side of the field, through the swathes of cut hay, to the tree where Riley was tied. Just beyond was a stone fence that separated the field from an old pasture which was growing up with brush and young pine. Riley was old and thin in 1939; his ribs stuck out and there was a sore on his left hip. My grandfather hated to work him, but he had no alternative, and he tried to make up to Riley with apples and sugar and praise.

Now, after he cooed a little at him, he untied Riley's rope and led him over to the big metal horse-rake, and backed him between the shafts. The mowing machine was next to it, leaning on its shafts like two long stiff arms, and the hayrack was just beyond.

My grandfather buckled the leather straps of Riley's harness, and I looked up to see Anson trudging across the field with a big pail of water. Riley leaned his neck into the pail and drank in long, rhythmic swallows. "You'll lose it, old baby, pulling out there in the sun," said my grandfather, and when Riley lifted his dripping jaws from the bucket, my grandfather climbed into the saddleshaped metal driver's seat, beside the handle which controlled the rake, and moved off to the cut hay.

He raked the hay into even strips, thirty feet apart, that crossed the field parallel to the road. After he had completed three trips up and down, Anson began to rake the strips into small haystacks. He used the bullrake, a great wooden rake about five feet wide with teeth a foot long and four inches apart. I took the tiny rake and trimmed around rocks and trees, getting the hay which my grandfather missed. When I had gathered enough to carry, I pulled it to the nearest strip or haystack. After I had finished with the trimming, I sat in the shade and chewed on pieces of grass.

There were no sounds but the whirr of an occasional car, and the shouts of my grandfather to Riley, "Whoa! Back! Get up!" The sun was high and I was already sweating, but the breeze cooled me off as I sat in the shade. I practiced noticing the details of texture and color around me. That summer I had a theory that if you looked at anything closely enough, it would be beautiful. I examined a blade of grass, its stringy construction and the layer of gray which seemed to underlie the green.

Soon little haystacks spotted the whole field. My grandfather finished making his long strips before Anson could pile more than a third of the hay, so he drew the rest into piles with the quicker horserake. It took about forty-five minutes to do all the raking.

My grandfather drove Riley next to the hayrack and climbed down from his metal perch. He took his cap off and wiped the sweat from his face and neck and head with a huge handkerchief. "Don't have any hair to catch the sweat with," he said, as I had heard him say often. Riley was finishing the pail of water. My grandfather sat down for a moment in the shade of the hayrack, until Anson walked up to us, pulling the bullrake. "Hot in the sun," my grandfather said. Then he stood and unfastened Riley from the rake and backed him into the shafts of the hayrack. "Time to pull some more hay, old Riley, old baby," he said, and he fastened the straps.

Anson climbed into the hayrack and clucked to get Riley moving toward the nearest pile of hay. "You'll rake after," my grandfather said to me. "You pull the bullrake after us now, and I'll show you what you'll be doing." We walked together to the first haystack. Anson handed my grandfather his pitchfork. My grandfather sank it expertly into the pile of hay and lifted most of it up to Anson, who placed it where he wanted it for his load. The rest of the haystack followed, leaving a scattering of hay too small to be picked up by a fork. Anson clucked, and Riley automatically began to move toward the nearest stack.

My grandfather let his fork drop. "Now this is what you do, boy," he said. He took the bullrake and in a few turns of the rake he had skillfully gathered the strands of hay left at the site of the pile. "See how to hold it?" he said. I thought I did, but when I first held the rake, he had to rearrange my hands for me. The difficulty was to keep the long teeth flat on the ground, neither pointing up and missing the hay nor pointing down and losing the hay in bounces. I managed to pull the wisp of hay over to the next pile, where Anson, who had jumped down from the wagon to pitch on, incorporated it in his next forkful. Then Anson climbed back up, my grandfather finished pitching the new pile on the rack, and I raked after, while they moved on. I was careful not to miss a single fragment, and I caught up with them just in time for my grandfather to pitch up what I had scavenged.

Anson packed and stowed and treaded the hay with the rote skill of forty years, building the load at the edges evenly back and front, so that the hay leaned out way over the rails, but was fastened securely by forkfuls treaded into the middle. The floor of the rack was only one plank wide near the front where it was cut by wells into which the wheels banked on a sharp turn. The single plank rested on the beam which was the wagon's main support, and to which the axles were attached. (I remember, from my early childhood, the late spring when my grandfather and Washington Woodward built the hayrack; the floor was thick boards bought from a lumber mill, but the rails were split birch, and the spokes which joined the rail to the floor were sticks with the bark still on them.) In loading the hay, it was tricky to cover the wells so that you could walk over them without losing hay, or even falling through yourself. At least it was tricky for me, when in later years I loaded for my grandfather.

Fifteen of the piles filled the old rack. Anson treaded the last two into the middle as binders, and we were ready to take the load home to the cow barn. I must have been hurrying with my raking, for I had forgotten to pay attention to what I was doing; when my rake stuck, I tugged at it and one of the foot-long teeth broke off. For a moment, in my chagrin, I wanted to hide it, but I knew that there would be no hiding it for long. I raked over to my grandfather. "I broke a tooth. The rake stuck in a skunk hole or something."

He laughed. "I reckon we'll have to take it out of your wages." He put the broken tooth in his long overall pocket and I went back to raking after the last pile. When I finished, my grandfather picked up the whole rake and swung it over his head, so that the hay didn't fall from it, and laid the final strip of hay across the back of the load, like a narrow fringe of curls on a girl's forehead.

We left the rake and the rest of the equipment behind us, along with considerable hay, and climbed into the wagon by the hub and the rim of a huge front wheel. For this ride, my grand-father handled the reins, while Anson dangled his legs over the back of the rack and sucked on a piece of hay. My grandfather said he loaded himself there to keep the rest of the hay in place. Only a few pieces of hay scattered behind us as we started home, leaving a trail which the cars soon dispersed. Riley walked de-liberately, and needed no direction. The cars zipped past us im-patiently, but we paid no attention to their haste. It was the op-posite of everything in Connecticut, to sit, sinking, in a pile of hay, while a bony old horse pulled a load of hay in a home-made rack along a New Hampshire road at three miles an hour. The smell of the hay was as great a pleasure as the softness of it, and I was full of the joy of haying.

My grandfather was happy, too. He kept talking about the significance of the day, as if he were one of the preachers of his childhood who read great meanings into common events. He talked about raking after when he was a boy, and pointed to fields across the valley in which he had pulled a bullrake. When we reached, finally, the yard in front of the farmhouse, old Ri-ley stopped without orders beside the kitchen door. My grand-mother and Aunt Caroline were sitting on the porch. "I'll start the coffee, Wesley," said my grandmother. "And how do you take to haying?" she said to me. "Did he do a man's work?" she asked my grandfather.

"I guess he *did*," said my grandfather. "And you see how much quicker we're through." Then he told me to go inside where it was cool, while he and Anson pitched off in the barn. Pitching off took only two men, and I was scarcely big or strong enough to be one of them.

Inside, my grandmother had drawn a pitcher of cold water from the deep well behind the house. The faucet was fed by a shallow well up the hill, and the water was not exceptionally good. The water from the deep well was the best I ever tasted, but it was hard to draw; we had to prime the pump and spill out several gallons before we had the real essence of it. The sides of the pitcher were frosted from the cold water, and I poured myself a tumbler and drank it in sips to prolong the pleasure. I waited in the dark, cool sitting room for my grandfather and Anson to finish pitching off. Then they came in to drink their coffee.

Soon we were off again, riding back to the widow's field in the empty hayrack. Anson drove, while my grandfather and I sat in the back and dangled our legs. We brought in two more loads that day, and I broke another tooth in the bullrake. After supper, my grandfather found a good piece of wood in the shed, and he sat on the chopping block and carved two teeth out of it, while I watched him. Even though I had made him extra work, I was happy because he was so happy. He told a dozen stories while he was carving. Anson was already up in his room over the kitchen. The light was out, and he was probably lying in the dark with his candy bars. It was really the start of something, and all that summer, six days a week except when it rained, I pulled a bullrake in my grandfather's fields.

IN LATER years, I learned to pitch on and to load, as well as to rake after, but I never learned to handle myself as well as my grandfather. He had his own particular pitchfork, which he had used as long as he could remember. Old black tape was wrapped around the wood where it joined the steel, to prevent a split from widening. The upper part of the handle, where his hands had slipped for many decades, shone as smooth as glass. He knew its moving balance as he knew how to walk or to milk a cow.

It was loading that I loved the most. I loaded when Anson had left the farm again, or when I could persuade him to trade with me and rake after. Of all the sensations retained from my summers, the most clear is this: I stand on top of a load of hay in the July sun; the load builds well out over the sides; my grandfather is catching his breath, so for a moment I stand still; I am high enough to catch the wind which is coming from the lake at my back, while the sun continually pushes down at me; the heat of the sun and the cool of the wind mingle, and neither is right without the other; a light sweat, always drying in the air, covers my bare back, and the chaff clings to it like the down on my face.

Each afternoon we pitched, loaded, and raked, and we usually brought in three loads to pack away in the dark barn. If it looked like rain we might hurry to bring in four, and keep the long line of Holsteins waiting outside the barn, milk dripping from their swollen udders. If we had to travel far for the hay, we might make two huge loads instead of three regular ones. In particular there was a single acre, beyond the boys' camp on the other side of the lake, which was solid with clover and sweet grass. Whenever we hayed there, my grandfather said, "Oh, but the cattle will love to eat *this* load!" I don't know why the land was so rich, but the tangle of growth was so thick that it was hard to walk through. And woodchucks had dug so many holes that we had to lead Riley among them by the bridle, walking in front to survey the mined land. It was so far away that we built the load far out on each side—nearly as wide as the dirt road we traveled on—and finished the acre in two afternoons of two loads each.

Sometimes our hay was poor, especially if it had stood too long uncut after it had turned ripe. The juice drained out, and in the winter the cattle would turn up their great pink-and-black noses at it. There was a meadow in back of the Whittemores' which was thick enough—your foot sank in the soft turf—but in which the weeds and the wild flowers grew as grossly as the pungent grass. Often when we brought in a load from the Whittemore meadow we stored it in the lofts of the sheep barn and spared the finicky cattle. For one thing, sheep didn't have milk to be off-flavor on the doorsteps of Manchester.

The greatest enemy was rain, unless there was no rain at all, and then drought was the enemy. What you wanted was a nice rainy Sunday, after you had cleaned a big field on Saturday afternoon, and before you cut another on Monday morning. When it rained and we had no hay down, I had a good lazy day and was glad of it; I read and wrote all day while my grandfather chopped wood and mended tools. But if hay was down when it rained, I was as gloomy as anyone. The stacks had to be torn apart and the hay spread to dry, and then turned over to dry on the other side, and then stacked again. Sometimes we would just finish stacking the hay a second time, when a thundershower would soak it again. If it was three times wet, even the best hay turned into a mudcolored and odorless straw. We could either throw it away or pass it off on the poor sheep.

We saw a lot of Merrimack County, haying, because my grandfather owned parcels of land in odd places, and because we sometimes took in someone else's hay, like the widow's. We talked in the rack, going and coming, and we talked even when we hayed. When I teased to pitch on, after Anson had left, it was partly because my grandfather would have more breath for talking if he loaded. But even while he pitched—and I stood above him taking in the sun—his soft voice kept on in the intervals between forkfuls. I heard so much about the past that the hayrack seemed a machine which took us into another century; or more as if it were big enough to contain the summers of his whole life at once. I lived with him when he was my age, and through all of his seven decades.

In the first years of haying, when Anson was with us, there was a part of me that assumed that I would spend the rest of my life haying. I could clearly see the three of us in the same fields of summer until the end of time, with the same bony Riley pulling the same frail hayrack—old man, half-wit, horse, and boy, locked in a scene where they repeated the same motions under the same skies. This tableau existed alongside the knowledge of death, that perpetual elegy which began earlier than I can remember, and which grew in the end to color everything I saw of the farm. The two feelings contradicted each other, but lived together like old brothers who had not spoken for forty years.

Anson and I were children together of the same old farmer. We giggled together when my grandfather joked. In order to bring Anson into the conversation, and probably in order to work off the irritations he must have felt, my grandfather often teased him. It was like teasing a four-year-old, because Anson never responded to a provocation until it had been rehearsed for him several times. The exchanges during our afternoons of haying followed a few known paths; every choice in the conversation limited the choices of the answer, until the final sentences resembled a *déjà vu*.

Anson would be loading while my grandfather pitched on, and my grandfather would say, "Now Anson, why can't you handle these forkfuls any faster? I'm spending all afternoon down here waiting for you to make room for me."

Anson would fume. "Yew jist sind up all yew kin sind up and I kin take ceer of what yew kin sind up."

So my grandfather, who had chosen the time for his teasing to coincide with our arrival at a big stack, would strain to lift an immense forkful onto the wagon. He would aim it so that the weight of it would catch Anson on the chest, staggering him back.

Anson would tum red and shout, "Yew don't have to knock me clean off the rack, yew old fuel!" (His special pronunciations were a delight to me. He could never say "garage," but had to say "aw mo-beel gaage." I used to puzzle myself inventing questions which would require him to use "garage" in the answer.)

My grandfather would laugh, and while Anson was still too enraged to dispose of the last forkful, he would send up another and another—until Anson humiliated himself by asking for a chance to catch up. Or Anson's abuse would grow wilder, and my grandfather would pretend to be angry. "Well, now, young man, we can't have you talking like that!" he would say, and he would stab his pitchfork into the ground and vault into the rack with sudden agility.

Anson would cower toward the opposite end of the wagon— though my grandfather had never touched him—and he would giggle and whine, "I never said nothin', Wesley."

When Anson pitched on and my grandfather loaded, which happened when his shoulder felt stiff, my grandfather had a trick which made Anson angriest of all. Anson's forkful of hay would come riding up, and my grandfather would plunge his own fork into the middle of it, twist it a little, and snap Anson's fork out of his hands. Then he would ask Anson innocently, "Why did you pitch up this old fork, boy?"

Anson would stare up at the rack empty-handed. "Wesley, yew old fuel, what yew take my fork for? I'm goin' to climb right up there and whup yew."

Once my grandfather answered, stiff shoulder or not, by making an immediate leap from the wagon to land with both forks in front of Anson. Anson turned as white as his skull, and he didn't even listen to my grandfather's, "Yes, sir. Here you are, sir. At your service, sir."

Most of the time we worked in silence or to the quiet narrative of my grandfather's stories, which Anson appeared to enjoy too. There were two of my grandfather's Lyceum poems which Anson preferred, and would beg him to recite. He could never remember the titles, but would ask for them by a word or two from somewhere in the poem. "Kin yew say the 'blue-eyed boy' one?' If my grandfather forgot a line or a stanza, Anson would object, but he could never help by remembering a word or a line.

It was in the winter, in 1942, that Lewis took Anson away for the last time. My grandmother wrote me in Connecticut to tell me, but said that she expected him to return in the spring. Then April came without Anson, and my grandfather spread cow manure on the garden and the corn field, and plowed it under, and planted his seed, and cultivated the growing fields—all by himself. By the time I arrived in June, he had already begun to hay alone.

I helped him, and the summers began when the two of us worked in the fields alone. We expected Anson to return until we heard Lewis's motive in taking him away, and then we knew that he would never work on the farm again. Anson had turned sixtyfive, and Lewis had filed his name for a pension. Anson owned no property, and the state sent him a check every month, which Anson signed and turned over to Lewis in return for his cot, his turnip greens, his salt pork, and a candy bar on Saturday nights in Franklin.

The summer of 1942 I stayed late, because a polio epidemic had made the Connecticut schools unhealthy congregations. We finished our haying the day before Labor Day. We had cut less than we wanted to, and a late spring in 1943 would mean buying hay. We had done only two loads a day, much of the time, because I was still not as strong as a man and because Riley was lame on two legs, and moved in a pain which it was pain to watch. His hair was patchy and his breath irregular and there were sores on his sides.

After the hay was stowed away, my grandfather cut the field corn and hauled it to the barn, and an ensilage crew came to the farm for one exciting day. They chopped it up in a putt-putting gasoline-driven machine and stowed it in the silo which was in- side the barn—next to the stall where old Riley had trouble ris- ing to his feet, now, after he had lain down. When they had left, my grandfather harnessed Riley once more and put the rack and the mowing machine away for the winter, under the dry roof of the shed next to the sheep barn. It was time to begin thinking about wood for the winter.

The next day my Aunt Nan, who was staying at the farm un- til school opened, suddenly became very interested in showing me the attic. It was a narrow loft above the room which we called the back chamber, which was also a place of storage. The attic had been filled when my mother was a little girl. We took a candle with us and set it carefully on an old, cracked plate. We climbed up the rickety ladder. In the gloomy hodge-podge we made out old toys, broken dolls, and the wooden model of a tugboat. Disorder heaped worn quilts on top of handleless chamber pots, broken stools beside cracked mirrors, and a pile of schoolbooks under a mound of old hats. I found a jack-in- the-box which still worked, though the cloth had worn from the spring. Wedging our way far in, digging through things saved like archaeologists searching for Troy, past bundles of let- ters and photographs and an album inscribed with poems, we saw in the far corner, its huge front wheel propped at an angle so that its spokes looked like an enormous spider web, an an- cient bicycle.

We must have looked around for an hour, carrying our can- dle and coughing in the dust we raised. Then I heard my grandmother call from the back chamber, standing at the foot of the ladder, "You going to come down now?" Aunt Nan picked up the candle, and I followed her down to the kitchen. Everyone was there, and no one would look at me. My grandfather was white. He took me into the living room while everyone else kept busy in the kitchen, and he told me that he had shot and buried Riley.

The horse's graveyard was across the railroad, on a sandy bank which overlooked the lake. My grandfather had loaded his shotgun with a slug, and had led the lame horse across the fields which Riley had plowed and reaped for so many years. He carried his gun and his shovel in his left hand, and he whispered love into the horse's ear. He had dug the grave while the old horse stood with rheumy eyes, and he had shot him so that he fell into the grave.

SIX

LUTHER, NANNIE, AND THE CALLERS

U NCLE LUTHER was my grandmother's older brother, and he and his sister Nannie, who was a few years older still, were part of the farm in my earliest summers. My young Aunt Caroline, who took long walks with me and told me stories from the *Odyssey*, was often there; and so was my younger Aunt Nan, with whom I competed as the new baby of the family. But I remember age more than youth from that time, when the old people in their last summers dozed on the porch and spoke slowly and intermittently about the farm's day.

When I knew him, Luther Keneston was minister of the South Danbury church. I heard him preach his elegant sermons without notes when he was more than eighty. He had been pastor of a large church in a town in central Connecticut and he retired at seventy in 1925, and returned to his home in New Hampshire. He bought the red cottage which he called Sabine, and which stood beyond the start of New Canada Road, between the farm and the church. It was so covered with ivy, in the later years, that you could barely see the wood until a tentacle of the plant pried loose another shingle. In the winter he slept at the farm, in a big room on the second floor which was always "Luther's room." After breakfast he would walk the half-mile to Sabine, light a wood fire with a dash of kerosene, and read and write all day beside the iron stove. In the summer he slept at the cottage, walking up the hill to the farm only for supper.

As a young man he had preferred books to farming. He learned Greek by himself, studying grammar by candlelight at night, and worked in his father's fields only when labor was short. His eyesight was poor, and his health was known to be delicate. In the world of his youth, there were two things a boy might do if he couldn't farm: he might teach or preach. He studied at Colby in New London, and when he graduated found jobs teaching at Andover, Wilmot, and New Boston. He spent six years teaching languages and other subjects, and he married another schoolteacher. Then he took orders as a minister of the Christian Church. Aunt Alice died before I was born, when their two children were barely out of school.

He was old when I knew him, stooped, with white moustaches and a white fringe of hair around his bald head. He carried a cane when he walked between Sabine and the farm. Once a week he abandoned the cane for an ancient motoring cap, and cranked the motor of his solid-wheeled, blue, window-curtained Studebaker. He picked up my grandparents and me at the farm, and drove us solemnly to church. He averaged fifteen miles an hour, and at least a quarter of the time he traveled on the left-hand side of the road. With his weak eyes glaring ahead, he bent fiercely over the blare of the horn: it was his only way to avoid an accident.

When I was too young to hay or to help with the chores, I used to tag after Uncle Luther when he was available. Often enough he would walk to the farm in time for a cup of coffee in the middle of the afternoon, and talk to me in the hour and a half before supper. I asked questions and argued about the answers. Once he said that everything God made had a purpose, so I drilled him about wasps. Frequently he told me jokes, laughing at them in an old, quavering laugh while I waited for him to explain the point to me. They were usually professional, and would begin, "A rabbi, a priest, and a minister went fishing..." The rabbi usually came out better than the priest.

He was vain, I suppose. Everyone made a good deal of him, and he expected to be served before the ladies at meals. Every year at Old Home Day, when most of the people from Wilmot and Wilmot Flat and West Andover and South Danbury and Potter Place gathered in the Methodist Camp Grounds, he gave a speech as the patriarch of the neighborhood, a perennial oldest inhabitant with the glory of the pulpit to add to the wisdom of age. He wrote poems which he printed as Christmas cards, and he even paid to collect a few of them in a pamphlet. In the last few years of his life he wrote a collection of prose sketches of his boyhood. When one publisher rejected it as "childish," he put it away, and it was burned by his orders at his death.

Some days he would walk up from Sabine with a new chapter finished, and he would read it to me as we sat on the porch before supper. I remember that I was startled to recognize Washington Woodward as a young man who leapt onto a horse to gallop in aid of a lady. I am sorry that I cannot read his stories now. Yet even then I think I was more interested in the reminiscences I prompted with my questions: when he wrote, he lapsed into the simple melodrama of the boys' stories he remembered from his childhood.

Once he told me that he had been my age during the Civil War. He remembered running to tell his father to hide, because he had heard that the drafting men from the government were coming to Danbury. If a farmer left his land to fight with the Union Army, his land grew up while he was gone, and there was no allowance to feed his wife. Uncle Luther remembered seeing wives plowing their kitchen gardens. Once a week his father trained with the local militia. When he marched off with his gun, his children were terrified and would not be comforted until he came home. They feared that he was going to "Virginia" or "Libby Prison"—those black words of the 1860s.

The greatest event in the month of August, when I was a boy, was Luther's birthday. The people of the parish gave a surprise party for him every year, and every year his astonishment, when the hoax was exposed and the celebration revealed, was greater than last year's. For a week before the party my head was full of secrets. My grandfather and I would take the old ice-cream maker from the back chamber, and my grandmother would clean it while Luther was at Sabine. The morning of the party we would pack it with salt and ice, and pour in the bowls of the mixed ingredients; then we would take turns at the handle until the liquid stiffened into ice cream, and a Model A would scurry into the yard and pick it up for delivery to the site of the party. My Aunt Caroline would usually arrange to be visiting with her car, and after supper she would suggest taking a ride. Uncle Luther would agree with an aggressive innocence. When we turned into a neighbor's drive, and saw the front lawn lighted with strings of lanterns, and striped with tables which were set with cakes and forks and plates, Uncle Luther would say, "What's this? What is Herbert Perkins up to tonight? It can't be a golden wedding." When he stepped out of the car, his parishioners would erupt from the house singing "Happy Birthday," and his face would show complete astonishment. When he made his speech in thanks for his birthday gift, he would say he was really fooled *that* year.

It was a church supper (after supper) in mid-summer. The children popped corn and ate too much ice cream and drank too much lemonade. The grown-ups stood talking in groups, stiff in their Sunday clothes, and drank coffee in the mild chill of the August evening. Someone might sing a song—"There's a Long, Long Trail A-Winding," or "Home on the Range," or "Old Black Joe"—and another minister from nearby, like Mr. Campbell from Wilmot Flat, might make a little speech about Uncle Luther. By nine o'clock I would lean sleepily on my grandfather in the back seat of Aunt Caroline's car, driving home in the dark to a feather bed.

The only event which could compare to Uncle Luther's birthday party was the Sunday School picnic, which came in July: egg sandwiches, peanut butter and jelly sandwiches, pineapple and cream cheese sandwiches; stuffed eggs, sweet pickles, and a burlap bag of peanuts in the shell; ice cream and cake and watermelon. Some sort of baseball game would occupy the big boys and the men, while the children competed in sack races, potato races, and jumping contests. Finally the children would gather under a maple beside the lake, at the far edge of Luther's sheep pasture where the picnic always took place, while Uncle

Luther told us a story. It was a fine way to spend a Saturday afternoon, but when the war came the picnics stopped, and they
never started again.

The last summer I knew Uncle Luther was 1941, the summer I was twelve. He had been ill in the winter, and had stayed
with his daughter in Brattleboro, Vermont. She drove him up
that August, so that he could spend a few weeks at Sabine. I
think he feared missing his birthday party. He tottered up to
the house on his cane as he always had, though it now took him
half an hour to walk it. Whenever he heard a car, he shuffled
into the sand at the side of the road and turned to peer at it until it passed. While he had been sick, Mr. Campbell had come
over from Wilmot Flat to preach to us, and the service had been
at two o'clock. Now while he was back, Uncle Luther insisted
on taking over. After all, the church had continued to pay him
five dollars a week, even when he was in Brattleboro. The only
thing he agreed to stop was his driving, and the old Studebaker
fell apart in a shed behind Sabine.

After supper, while my grandfather was finishing his chores,
Uncle Luther and I sat on the porch in the buggy twilight. He
never started a conversation, but he liked to have me ask him
questions. My grandmother urged me to talk to him, because
it improved his disposition. I asked him about the country he
had walked through when he was young, and he gave long accounts of places and people dead or forgotten. He told me about
a place he called God's pool, which I was to see with my grandfather years later. Twice that August I walked down to Sabine
and talked with him. My grandmother was continually nervous
that he would have a stroke there, and that we wouldn't know.
We sat among his books and papers and dirty coffee cups and
talked as we did in the evenings.

He died that winter in Vermont, eighty-six years old. I felt
little sadness when he died. He was so old that it had almost
seemed agreed by everybody, himself included, that he should
die that winter. I never felt really intimate with him, as I did
with my grandfather. He was always a little frail and strange.

I remember one afternoon when I was six or seven, and was sitting in the back seat of a car with him and holding his hand; I discovered that if I pressed the flesh in the back of his hand, behind the interval between the thumb and the forefinger, the dent stayed after I had removed my finger, and the flesh only very slowly reassumed its former shape. I remember experimenting over and over again with this phenomenon, never conscious that he might realize what I was doing, or that he would care if he did.

His sister Nannie was older than he, and since she died in 1938 I remember little about her. In fact it is the summer of her death that I chiefly remember. From my grandfather's histories I learned that she was a schoolteacher before she was married to a man who was a station agent for the Boston and Maine. She had a daughter and a house, and then her husband dropped dead while shoveling snow in front of his station. She went back to teaching, the stern disciplinarian whom my mother and my aunts remember from their one-room school. Though she married again later in life, and lost her husband again, she changed little after her first widowhood. As I remember her face from my earliest childhood, her mouth was perpetually curved in a bitter new-moon.

She had begun to go blind when I first knew her. The little cottage in which she lived, three hundred yards from the farmhouse along the road toward the West Andover depot, was so familiar to her that she could find her way about it easily, but she found it difficult to light the stove and to cook. My grandmother feared that she might fall and break her hip, or set the house on fire. Then Aunt Nannie became convinced that someone was trying to trick her; she put things in memorable places and when she went back for them they were gone. She harangued my grandmother with endless accounts of this mischief, and one day revealed that it was a cousin of her first husband's who was doing it, a woman who had been rude to her fifty years before, and who had died at the turn of the century.

My grandmother persuaded her to move to the farm, and

argued with her about the persecutions. Aunt Nannie settled in happily, sleeping on a cot in the parlor, and for a while her delusions ceased. Then one night my grandparents woke to hear her screaming obscenities, and when they rushed into her room with a light she was sitting up in bed with her long gray unbraided hair streaming back over her white nightgown, her blind eyes staring at the wall and her toothless mouth spitting anathemas. What puzzled my grandfather was her vocabulary.

The doctor diagnosed senile dementia, and suggested that she go to an old person's home, but my grandmother didn't want to send her away; she argued that a public place was uncomfortable and a private one expensive, but it was really a matter of principle with her: it was her place to nurse her sister. Two months later I arrived for the summer. I was nine years old, and everyone explained very carefully what had happened, but I remember her shrieks, more than twenty years later, as if I were still sleeping a wall away from them. She was in pain, and she imagined that she was being tortured. I was only allowed to visit her in the rare moments of calm and clarity. I would be led in to see her stretched out on her cot, as white as her bedclothes, while her open eyes wandered and she murmured, "Donnie, Donnie, Donnie." Then my grandmother would motion me to say "Goodbye" and go.

Every day I could hear her cursing my grandmother, whom she called "Old Kate." She complained that she was being made to sleep on a pile of cordwood in the shed. Her back must have hurt her continually. One time when young Aunt Nan was visiting, she said to Nannie, "Stand up. I'll take you to a good bed." She helped Nannie up and then walked her around the parlor while my grandmother smoothed the sheets. Aunt Nan was saying, "This is the kitchen. Watch out for the stove. Step down into the sitting room. Here we go. Now you can lie down." Nannie lay down on her cot and said thank you and went to sleep.

Another time she complained to my grandmother that she never saw Kate and Wesley Wells any more. My grandmother quickly said that she thought she could arrange a visit. All day she kept Nannie in order by promising that Kate and Wesley would come by after supper. When the chores were done that evening, Old Kate told Nannie that the Wellses were just arriving. She stepped into the sitting room and put on a hat and re-entered with my grandfather. Nannie cried with joy to be with them. Nannie talked with them for an hour, clear and rational except that she complained of the people she lived with. But the next morning, when my grandmother asked her if she would like to go and live with the Wellses, Nannie screamed abuse at her and shouted that she *was* living with the Wellses.

She died two days before the hurricane. They buried her in the rain, and drove home only hours before the wind covered the clapboards at the side of the house with the leaves of my grandfather's flattened field corn. The same wind tilted the huge elm on the hill near the barn onto the roof of the old outhouse, and uprooted the forest of rock maple which I saw seven years later when we went blueberry picking. I was in the fifth grade in Connecticut then, and I hid from the same wind.

LUTHER AND Nannie—and Washington Woodward, whom they had known as a younger brother—were the old people I knew best after my grandparents. Others were our callers. On Sunday afternoons we sat reading in the sitting room and wondered who would come. Often there were so many that we emptied the dining room and kitchen of their wooden chairs, and the sitting room was as crowded as a theater. And it was not only Sundays. The late light of the evenings of early summer invited people to ride in their automobiles, and they gave themselves reasons by paying visits. We all sat together in the slant sun of the sitting room, or we fanned away insects on the porch, while Mount Kearsarge gathered the pink sunset in the distance.

I liked it especially when Gene and Lottie came to call. Lottie was my grandfather's older sister, and Gene Currier had been his friend at the hame shop before they became brothers-in-law. Gene was tiny and quick. He was older than my grandfather, and I remember him snatching flies out of the air with his fast hands when he was more than eighty. He talked as quickly as he moved, and his conversation was freckled with small profanities. My grandmother always complained about his swearing after he left, and looked sideways at me to see if I had been affected. He and my grandfather hilariously reminisced, reminding each other of a new story with every story they finished. I sat on the floor of the porch beside my grandfather's rocker and dangled my legs into the border of flowers, dreaming and listening to the rumble of old voices and old laughter.

Lottie was beautiful. My grandfather remembered her as a tomboy who could carry a hundred-pound sack of grain under each arm when she was fifteen, and wrestle her brothers onto their backs. When she was seventeen, she became the beauty of the back country where they lived, and the blacksmith's house was suddenly crowded with suitors. My grandfather remembered an evening when a cat leapt onto Lottie's lap, and a boy blurted, "Oh, I wish I was that cat!" and ran outside in embarrassment. When he retold the story, Lottie blushed again. Usually the two women chatted together—not listening to the men's stories—about weather and canning and the diseases of their friends and the new babies of their descendants. They never talked about the past as the men did.

Gene was a chicken farmer. He kept four hundred hens until he was eighty-five, and carried water to them in two twenty-quart pails. One day when he returned from the watering and graining, he found Lottie slumped over her sewing on the dining-room table, dead in the middle of a stitch. It was in May, and my grandmother wrote me. That summer Gene came over alone, and usually brought with him a batch of doughnuts which he had cooked himself on the wood stove of his solitary kitchen.

There were other old people who came three or four times a year, cousins who lived in Enfield or Salisbury or Canaan, and who made the family visit an impressive occasion. Other people came annually, mostly men and women who had moved south to the cities, but who returned to New Hampshire in their summer vacations. Other visitors were stranger still. We might be sitting on the porch after dinner on Sunday when a new car would slow down and enter the U-shaped driveway. All our eyes would strain into the darkness of the front seat as the car stopped in front of us. Then, "Ethel and William!" my grandfather might say, and the couple would edge out of the car and everyone would embrace, and talk at once, and then drink coffee for half an hour before Ethel and William moved on to their next old friend.

The people who returned from the city drove big cars and were dressed in city clothes, but when they rocked on the porch in the afternoon they could only talk about the air of the country, and reminisce over boyhood, baseball, and courting. Sometimes they seemed nervous, and they boasted about a house they had bought or a trip they had taken to Florida. Or they remarked on the hard life of a farmer, and contrasted their own forty-hour week. My grandfather would simply smile and nod until they had finished, and then bring them back to story-telling again.

Constant brief callers were my grandfather's brothers' daughters, Audrey, Edna, and Martha, who lived nearby with their husbands and families and often drove in the yard to chat without leaving the car. But the steadiest callers were neither old people nor family. Enoch and Margaret Bunwell moved into the Blakeley place when the roof was almost falling in, and they lived there for years without touching it. My grandfather said he believed that when it rained they slept in the outhouse, which had tarpaper on the roof. The Bunwells came from Vermont and were no relation, but they were very kind to my grandparents. Enoch stopped by every morning in his pickup truck to see if everyone was all right, and slowed and tooted his horn as we sat on the porch in the evening. If anyone was sick, he stopped twice a day.

When they first arrived, Enoch asked if he could have a dozen eggs every two days. My grandfather sold eggs and fresh milk to his neighbors. Enoch picked up the eggs regularly, but never asked if he might pay for them, and my grandfather never mentioned it. That winter Enoch sought out my grandfather. "How you fixing to get your wood?" he asked. Each winter my grandfather hired men to cut timber and saw it into cordwood. Then he would let it weather for twelve months until it was ready for the stove.

"I figured I'd hire it done, the way I've been doing."

Enoch, who didn't talk very much, shook his head. "Reckon I can do that," he said. He did, and his work was barter for the eggs, though neither man said as much. I wondered if Enoch bartered for many things. He had no steady job, but worked from place to place, chopping wood or carpentering or cleaning a well. Then, like other young men who stayed on in the country, he found steady work as caretaker and odd-jobber for the summer people, looking after their houses in the winter, and mowing grass and doing chores in the summer.

Often in the evening Enoch and Margaret and their four boys called. Sometimes it was a yard visit, and we would lean in the windows of the old truck and talk. Of course the four boys sat in the back, where they bounced among pieces of chain and broken shovels. Other times we all sat in the living room. I used to try to make the boys talk. They all stared at me and appeared to follow every word with great concentration, but none of them would ever speak. "Shy," said my grandmother, who was secretly worried about their intelligence. They made a grotesque family group, the six of them. The four boys sat staring with their mouths open, the rest of their faces oblongs of bone. They looked like their father except that they had noses. Enoch had nearly no nose at all. His eyes were small and sunk deeply into his face, of which the brow and chin jutted equally. From the side his face was concave.

Margaret looked more nearly human, but she was fat. She was not very tall, and she weighed 280 pounds. Her fat spread in every direction, with a variety that seemed ingenious. Even the top of her skull was fat. When she moved, she groaned and grunted with the labor of lifting her pork-barrel legs. When she sat on the sofa, her thighs spread over it like water in a balloon; her skirt tightened and revealed the pumpkins which were her knees. A torrent of chins rushed onto her breast, which led like a river to the great ocean of her stomach. Her arms sagged at her sides like continents.

Conversation wasn't much with Enoch and Margaret. My grandmother and Margaret might talk about weather and gardens, but my grandfather and Enoch and I had little to say. If you said to Enoch, "I figure Hitler is going to beat us in Europe and the Japanese will invade California," he would blink for a few seconds and then answer, "Mought be." He didn't seem aware of anything outside his car and his work of the day.

After the war, when he had his new job, they traded the 1934 truck for a 1942 model, and drove to Franklin every Saturday night for a good time. Enoch would listen to the men in the barber shop, and Margaret would shop or sit in a movie. Each of the boys would have fifty cents to spend on candy, and when they returned at ten-thirty, each of the boys would be sick in the back. When Enoch took us to church on Sunday, my grandparents sat up front and I squatted on a box in the back. The smell of that back is one of my less pleasant remembered sensations.

Enoch and Margaret bought a washing machine on time, and then a refrigerator with a large freezing compartment, and then a freezer. Every December Enoch shot a deer, and they ate venison hamburgers until the Fourth of July. They bought a television set, and the highest aerial Franklin could provide, and then a new used truck, and then a combination radio and record-player, and then they traded in the old washing machine for an automatic model. It was all on time, and every week a new round of payments was a new crisis. Enoch was always looking for evening work, or a bit of fixing to be done on a Sunday. My grandfather figured that he worked a ninety-six-hour week, and that each venison hamburger cost about $3.40. My grandfather joked about Enoch, but I could tell that Enoch puzzled him. Here was a man who didn't know what he was doing; here was a man who lived and worked to pay interest on things he didn't need; who had no interest in land, or in animals, or in the quality of his work, or in the education of his children, or in the politics of his nation. Enoch wasn't like my grandfather, or like the other old people with whom my grandfather had grown up, the last of whom called on us now in the summers.

SEVEN

THE LONG DAY

IF THERE were no callers in those long evenings, we sat in the
living room by ourselves. I would be reading the novelist I
had most recently discovered; my grandfather would be going
over a favorite Joe Lincoln or Zane Grey or Grace Livingston
Hill for the ninth time; and my grandmother would sew or knit
in the bad light at the end of the sofa. My grandfather would
snicker over Joe Lincoln, grin with excitement at Zane Grey, and
cluck sympathetically with Grace Livingston Hill. Every few
minutes my grandmother would say something which indicated
her thoughts: "Isn't it peculiar the Bucks didn't stay to Sunday
School?" or, "Suppose Danny Bussell will settle down when he
gets back from the Army?" My grandfather and I would make an
interested noise and keep on reading.

After we listened to the news at nine o'clock, on the radio
which stood like a chest of drawers in a corner of the living
room, we moved to the kitchen for a snack before bed. We
stood on the bare boards of the floor and talked about that day
and the next. My grandmother drank a glass of Moxie, I had
pie and a piece of rat cheese, and my grandfather swallowed a
small bowl of bread and milk. His soft voice teased my grandmother, and she pretended to be irritated. If he remembered a
story, as he often did when he had been reading, he would tell
it while my grandmother muttered disapprovingly about the
conduct of the people. We were in bed by nine-thirty. I slept in
the bedroom beside theirs, and I heard them whisper together
in bed for a few minutes after a silent space while they said their
prayers. I read until I was sleepy, which was usually before ten.

When I woke every morning, I knew what the day would provide. The six days of work were followed by a Sunday when we went to church, read books, and received callers. The farm had an order to it, for the animals had to be fed and the vegetables had to be weeded and the hay had to be cut for winter. Everything done was part of a motion we didn't control but chose to implement—a process of eating, mating, and dying. I liked the sense of necessary motion. The farm was a form: not like a set of rules on a wall, but like the symmetry of winter and summer, or like the balance of day and night over the year, June against December. My grandfather lived by the form all his life, and my summers on the farm were my glimpse of it.

The summer days were the ones I knew, not the winters when he chopped wood, and when he hauled thick slabs of ice from the lake to his ice house, where he kept them covered with sawdust for the milk of the summer. School in Connecticut kept me from the farm in winter. We drove up to New Hampshire each year on the week-end before Christmas, to celebrate an early holiday with my mother's family. It was a special occasion, and I saw none of the real days of the farm. But when I was very little and school didn't matter, I used to spend a week there with my mother before Christmas. I remember that my grandfather wanted me to go fencing with him, and my grandmother said I was too young. My grandfather said he wouldn't go if I didn't go, taking his stand with a mock childishness. My grandmother relented, and we spent a long morning walking on the edge of the cow pasture, while my grandfather chopped branches from trees to plug holes in the fence, and told me stories and poems.

When I was going to college in Massachusetts, I came up several times for week-ends in the winter. The house looked different in the deep snow which was always piled around it. The green shutters, which you hardly noticed among the leaves of summer, stood out against the whiteness of the world. Smoke rose like feathers over the house from the good logs burning in the kitchen range, and from the Glenwood stove in the living room, which was removed in the summer. The dining room kept warm because it lay between the kitchen and the living room, but my bedroom, which was at the front end of the house, was as cold as a snowdrift. A hot-water bottle and a pile of quilts, and I snuggled deep in the down of the mattress with comfort. In those winter mornings, I would wake at six to hear my grandfather fussing with the stoves, lighting the kerosene which rumbled like thunder and started the logs blazing. When he had set both fires, he would crawl back into bed for a few minutes. In the end they would both dress by the warmth of the sitting-room stove.

A few minutes later, my grandmother would call "Coffee's ready," and I would stumble from the bedroom to the kitchen carrying my clothes and would let them warm on a rack over the stove while I drank my first cup in my pajamas. By that time my grandfather would have finished his cup—he could drink boiling water, I think—and would be milking already up in the dark barn.

In the summer my grandfather's day started much the same. After he had milked the cows, he let them out to pasture and cleaned the tie-up. When all the milk had strained into the big cans, he would hoist them by a crane into the trough in the milk room where chunks of the winter's ice floated all summer long. While the milk was cooling he came down the hill from the barn for breakfast, and afterward he might sharpen his scythe and the blades of the mowing machine against the haying of later in the day.

I remember a day which began early for me. It was early July, in 1944. I was working at my poems in my room, just after waking, when I heard my grandfather call from the barn to my grandmother. Then, after she had time to stick her head out the door and put her hand behind her ear, I heard him shout, "Tell Donnie to come up here. There's something he ought to see."

I was already in the living room when my grandmother called me. "What is it?" I asked her.

"I don't know," she said. "I guess he wants to surprise you."

I walked outside. The trumpet at the boys' camp across the

pond suddenly broke into reveille, so I knew that it was a quarter to seven. My grandfather was standing in the big doors of the barn, in back of the hayrack which we had emptied the day before. When I was near, he pointed at the barn floor, and I saw a patch of brown fur. I leaned over it and saw that it was a fox, perfectly still, its eyes open.

"Dead?" I said.

My grandfather nodded. "And still warm," he said. I knelt and touched the fur. The ribs stuck out on the skinny body, and I felt the slight warmth.

"What do you suppose happened?" I said.

"Maybe he was alive when I came up here first," said my grandfather. "I was in the tie-up until just now. I'm glad he didn't get into your chickens. I reckon he felt sick, and wandered in here on the straw to die in a bit of comfort."

He was a handsome little thing. Of course it was summer and the pelt was no good to anyone. "Shall I bury him?" I said. One of the chores I had assumed was grave-digging. I buried the cats or hens who were run over, and the woodchucks or hedgehogs we managed to shoot.

"I guess so," said my grandfather. "Show him to your grandmother on the way."

He went back to the tie-up to finish his milking. I took my pitchfork from the hayrack and lifted the young fox and most of his straw bed, and carried him in front of me down the hill. My grandmother, who had been watching, came out of the kitchen. "What do you have there?" she asked. I showed her and we marveled at it together. Then I took a shovel from the shed and buried the fox in the garden, where we had already pulled up early peas to contribute to next year's table. The day had already started by that time. Poems could wait until tomorrow. I decided to feed the chickens.

That summer I took care of two hundred baby chicks. In the morning I let them out and fed them and in the afternoon I brought them grain and water again. At night when it got dark, I closed them in their wire cage to protect them from the foxes and the skunks. Now I filled a pail with grain and carried an empty bucket for water in the other hand. I let the chickens out of their little house and poured the grain evenly in their feeders. I filled my pail at the watering trough and used a little of the water to clean their dirty drinking apparatus, and then filled it with the rest. The two hundred chickens gabbled around me, and fought for places at the grain feeders.

Across the pond another trumpet call sounded as I crossed the road and climbed to the grain shed with my empty pails. One of the earliest things I remember about the farm took place at that grain shed. I must have been about five, and was lifting handfuls of grain and letting them sieve through my fingers. Inevitably some grain spilled on the floor and my grandfather asked me to stop. I persisted and he told me again. Finally I provoked him into shouting at me, and was so astonished when he raised his voice that I ran crying all the way down the hill into the house.

I set my pails in the shed, and walked into the barn. My grandfather's pitchfork was lying in the bottom of the hayrack, and I remembered that mine was still down by the shed. I ran down the hill and walked back up with it. I looked in the horse stall. Roger, who was Riley's successor, looked at me as if I might have something material to offer, and turned away when I only chattered at him.

"You there, Donnie?" called my grandfather. I walked into the tie-up and lifted a three-legged stool from a peg on the wall and sat down near the cow my grandfather was milking. The steady alternation of the thick streams of milk beat its rhythm in the pail. My grandfather's cheek pressed into the cow's side and the big Holstein idly swished its tail at flies. "How did Katie like the fox?"

"She said she'd never known of such a thing before," I said.

"I don't guess so either, not on the barn floor. Of course, an animal can die anywhere it has a mind to. Ben Peabody—I've told you about him—had an old spotted dog that he was mighty fond of. Come one day and the old dog was gone, and Ben figured he'd gone off in the woods to die. A week or so later and

Ben figured he'd died a sight closer, but he couldn't find him. He almost tore the house down, I guess. It smelled worst in the parlor, and he come close to taking out the floor. One day he tore the cardboard out of the front of his fireplace, that was all filled in, and found the poor critter there. Ben said he always knew the critter was smart, but he never expected him to be able to pull the cardboard in after him."

I laughed with him, and he wrinkled up his nose. "My, my. Old Ben didn't smell too good himself, but my, my."

For a while we said nothing. I watched a spider carrying a fly in his web against the whitewashed ceiling above me. My grandfather was concentrating on his milking, stripping the last ounces of frothy milk from the huge udder. "Tell me 'Lawyer Green,'" I said.

He smiled and was pleased. "Just wait till I empty this," he said. I followed him into the milk room and watched him pour the pail of milk into the big funnel of the strainer which was fixed over the mouth of the milk can. We could hear it dripping through slowly as we walked back into the tie-up. "Lawyer Green," he said. "Now how does that begin?" And before I could tell him he had started.

Lawyer Green was a poem about a boy with green skin who was ridiculed in the town of his birth, and who returned in triumph as a great lawyer. It took four or five minutes to recite. My grandfather always told it seriously, with long pauses for dramatic effect. If he had not been milking, he would have made wide gestures with his hands. Now he had to content himself with leaning back his head, rolling his eyes and making his mouth an O of surprise.

He knew many more pieces, and once he had started he would continue through a fair number of them. Every summer he seemed to remember a new one from the time in his youth when he had memorized so many to speak at the Lyceum. If he thought of one in the winter, he saved it for me like a present. For many years he had spoken them to no one. The Lyceum— where the farmers had acted, debated, and listened to speeches—had vanished by the time my mother was a girl, and my grandfather had gone without an audience until I came along.

The next cow was the last one. It was the Jersey, who gave less milk than the Holsteins, but a milk which was half cream. There were only seven cows now, and the bull which the butcher loaned him each year. (My grandfather fattened the bull while he used him for stud.) We walked to the milk shed and poured the cream in the pail with the strainer on top.

When the cows were let out and the tie-up cleaned, and while the milk was cooling, we came down the hill arm in arm to eat a breakfast of oatmeal and fried eggs and slices of bread. I finished with a piece of custard pie. My grandparents talked intermittently about the fox, and about other animals which had appeared and disappeared strangely. Then my grandmother said, "There isn't a great deal of wood, Wesley."

My grandfather nodded. "We have a lot of hay down now," he said, "up at Crumbine's, and I don't want to get too far ahead for fear of rain. I thought I'd chop some wood instead of mowing this morning, and maybe do one or two other things. I'd rather not cut any more hay today."

I walked out to the woodshed with him. The cordwood had been split and sawed into chunks short enough for the stove, but he split each half log into two or four smaller pieces to make the wood burn better for the kind of quick, hot fire you wanted in the summer. I liked to watch him chop wood, though I couldn't do it myself; it was the only one of my grandmother's nervous prohibitions which we accepted. I loved the brief solid sound his ax made breaking through a chunk of pine and pounding against the rock maple of the chopping block. I had to stand right in front of him, and not too close, for the chopped sticks flew off sometimes like surprised birds.

This morning, when I had seen my grandfather dispose of a dozen logs, I interrupted his rhythm to say, "I think I'll go do some reading," and he smiled as I left him. My bedroom was remote from the kitchen where my grandmother worked. On the old brown table were my typewriter, the pile of papers which were my poems, and a heap of books. The room was my sanctuary. There was a lot of time on the farm when I couldn't have been much help to anybody, though I could have found work if I had wanted it enough. At home things always pushed at me, and I never felt as quiet and meditative as I felt on the farm. I took advantage of the difference. Long mornings I spent reading, and dropping my book to daydream. Sometimes I left the room and wandered in the pasture, or in some cut hayfield near the house. I remember lying in the grass on my back many hours even when I was twelve and thirteen, watching the clouds and trying to make it all into stanzas.

That morning I sat at my desk with my books for an hour. I read quickly and badly, still feeling that I had so much to read that it mattered terribly to read four pages instead of three. Outside my windows the shade of the weed trees was dense, and the noise of a car slurring past was the only distraction. Then I heard voices and looked up to see a troop of the boys from the camp as they marched past my window in the road, double file. They wore uniforms, and marched almost in step, and I saw counselors with whistles at front and rear. They were taking a hike. They were seeing the country. It was the way the boys I knew in Connecticut spent their summers, first as campers and now as assistant counselors. Their bugles and uniforms and square cabins and dining hall and ordered games could only re-mind me of the blocks at home. While I was looking up from my book, I heard a light tapping at my door. "Gram?" I said.

She opened the door. "You busy?" she said.

"No."

"Gramp thinks you might like to have a buggy ride," she said, and grinned. It was so rare to hitch a horse to the buggy now, that she knew I would be excited to do it.

I ran from the house up the hill to the barn and found my grandfather backing Roger into the shafts of the two-seat-ed buggy. My grandfather was smiling too. "Do you want to come?" he said.

"Sure I do!" I said. "Where to?"

"We've got to get us some salt. I've called Herbert Perkins at Cilleyville three times, but he can't say when he'll get here with the truck. So I reckon we'll go get some. Summer is the time the critters need the salt." He was fastening the harness. The buggy was covered with dust and spider webs, and looked as if it had not been used for ten years, though I had sat in it for the short ride from the depot only four weeks before. Even when I was a small child, the cloth on the seat had been torn and I had absently pulled the horsehair out of it. My grandfather led Roger and the buggy in front of the kitchen, and my grandmother came out with her broom and cleaned away some of the debris. We climbed up, called goodbye to her, and started off at a good pace. Roger wasn't used to so light a load.

My grandfather pulled his watch from his trousers pocket. "Ten o'clock," he said. "An hour there and an hour back. You shouldn't be late for your dinner, boy!" My appetite was always good, and I heard a lot about it. "Time was," he went on, "that I did the round trip in an hour and ten minutes. That was when Riley was young." He began to laugh, in a teasing way. "Do you know when you made this trip the last time, Donnie?"

I thought for a second. "With Riley," I said.

He laughed. "Yes, and he wasn't so young then, but my, how he kicked up the dirt. You must have been six years old. You got so mad at Riley because he kept kicking dirt in your face. You never thought to get mad at me because I kept twitching the reins to keep him going fast." He laughed and laughed. "I'm afraid old Roger couldn't do that for us," he said.

Roger, who had started by trotting, slowed to a walk in a hundred yards. We passed Aunt Nannie's old cottage, and climbed the little hill past a side road that cut over to the camp. At the top of the rise we could see ahead to the Whittemores' farm. On our left were only their old sap house and the water pipe which ran above ground in the rocky pasture. On our right was their big barn, painted red by the makers of Beech Nut Chewing Tobacco and advertising that product. Beyond it was the low white farmhouse.

Once I had walked out in back of the farm with one of the brothers and I had seen that the back of the house, which was only fifty yards from the railroad, was unpainted. It seemed indecent, like a hole in pants, and the whole farm was shabby under a light and hasty front of upkeep. Underneath the Beech Nut paint, the timbers of the barn were rotten. Bits of machinery rusted in the tall grass next to the road. In the parlor of the house where guests were taken, the furniture was comfortable and clean; a primitive painting of the farm hung over the closed fireplace, left as payment for board and room by an itinerant painter-tramp. But if you looked into other rooms you saw the stale debris of poverty.

The reason for it sat in the front yard as we rattled up. Charlie Whittemore was sitting in a straight-backed chair on the stingy grass of his lawn. He was incredibly thin. His wrists hung out of his sleeves like pale straws, and his legs as they showed in his faded overalls were as narrow as bones. His face looked glazed with disease and his gray cheeks sunk in as far as his eyes. His adam's apple stuck out in his turkey's throat as if it stretched the skin to the point of pain. His chest sank backward beneath his bony shoulders. He didn't look as if he could speak. He looked more like a mummy dead four thousand years than a living man. But he had looked like that for as long as I could remember.

My grandfather pulled Roger into the sand between the road and the grass, and said, "Whoa. Good morning, Charlie."

Charlie cleared his throat. He didn't try to stand. "Good morning, Wesley. Donnie. How you been?"

"Tolerable, Charlie. How you been?"

"Not so good. All right, though. Where you going?"

"To Perkins's in Cilleyville. To get some salt. Would you like to come for the ride?" I wondered where my grandfather intended to fit Charlie. The two-seater seemed full enough.

"Can't, Wesley." He made the sound of clearing his throat again, for a long time. "I can't take the jiggling. Thank you."

"All right, Charlie. I guess we'd better get on."

"Goodbye."

"Goodbye."

We started again, along the flat half-mile which separated us from Henry Powers' store and post office.

"How long has Charlie been sick?" I asked.

My grandfather thought. "About twenty-five years," he said. "Goodness, I hadn't thought it was so long. The farm was some different, before. He worked very hard. Folks always said he was stingy, but I reckon he worked himself harder than he worked one of his hired hands. Something happened to one of his lungs, and the other isn't so good."

The Whittemores' nearest neighbors were the Bradburys, whose unpainted house and barn we passed next. It always looked as if no one lived there. Holes in the windows were stuffed with yellow paper, and the door was perpetually ajar. The Whittemores and the Bradburys didn't get on, but then William Bradbury didn't get on with anybody. Once William had been a good farmer like Charlie, but he took to drink in the farm depression after the first war. Mary Bradbury went to church most Sundays, a stiff Christian, but William seldom showed his face outside his parlor, and the two of them lived on the eggs which Mary's chickens laid. They had some money from their son in the Army, and some from their daughter Hester who taught school in Franklin, but they never had much because William spent it on liquor.

Of all the younger people I met in New Hampshire, I really knew Hester best. She was only eight years older than I and she was the only person younger than my grandparents who seemed to love New Hampshire the way I did. On the rare occasions when we met, we talked about the farms and the woods and the cellar holes which nobody else seemed to notice.

We drove past Henry's store, waving to him where he rocked on the porch, and turned down the hill and crossed the railroad track. We passed the ruins of the general store where my grandfather had clerked, and turned off the macadam onto a dirt track which I knew as the Cilleyville road. When I was a child I could hardly believe that there was such a place as Cilleyville, even though my great-great-grandmother had been born a Cilley herself.

The road was empty and Roger walked stolidly along it. My grandfather talked to me every time he thought of something. We passed the ruin of a great system of cages, and he told me about the fox farm which had thrived there a decade earlier. We passed a road which was all but grown over, and he recited the names of friends who had lived on it. "My father had a friend lived there named Percy Green. Old Percy had a rooster he called Abe Lincoln. He was a Democrat, and he said this rooster made more noise than any creature in Christendom, but he wasn't much good at laying eggs."

To get to Perkins's we had to cross a covered bridge, the last one for miles around. Then we made a sharp turn and drove into the yard of the granary, which was full of trucks and cars. A buggy was already so rare that people stared at us, but there was still a hitching post and we tied Roger to it and went inside the office to get our bag of salt. "Hello, Herbert," said my grandfather to a man with steel-rimmed glasses.

"Wesley," said Perkins. "Is this your grandson?"

"Lucy's boy." My grandfather nodded. I was looked over.

"I can see some Lucy in him," said Herbert. "I guess you want your salt."

"Yep," said my grandfather.

Herbert walked from the office by a side door and reappeared with a sack of salt. "You tied up out here?" he said. My grandfather nodded. Herbert carried the salt to the buggy and tucked it behind the seat. "I don't like to make you waste your morning, Wesley," he said.

"It's good to get out like this," said my grandfather. "The boy hasn't been out in the buggy like this for a year or two, have you, Donnie? Except for when he comes in on the Peanut."

"No," I said, "not for three years, I guess."

"And besides," said my grandfather, "we've got too much hay cut on the ground already."

Herbert was edging back toward his office. "Well, good-bye, Wesley. Best to Kate. I'll bill you for this when I bill you for grain."

We untied the reins and climbed back into the seat. In a moment we had crossed the covered bridge and were ambling along the flat Cilleyville road toward home. I asked my grandfather how long it had taken him to drive to Franklin by buggy, and the question started him recollecting the longest buggy rides of his life. He told me, too, about driving cattle for three and four days to market, over the dirt roads of his boyhood. Then he said, "I suppose it was your grandmother who used this buggy more than anyone."

"When?" I said. I had never known her to handle a horse. It didn't occur to me that she would ever leave the house by herself.

"She drove a smart trap when she taught school," he said, "but that was only for three years. When she sold millinery, she took trips every day in the spring with her new hats, and she covered many miles in those years."

Then I remembered the millinery and even a little about the trips in the spring. For fifteen years while my mother was growing up, my grandmother turned the front parlor into a millinery shop. There was no place for fourteen miles around to buy a hat. Sears and your Singer might do for dresses, but hats were more of a problem. Every spring my grandmother took a trip to Boston to buy hats and to learn the new styles. When she came back she made as many as she could, and her stock included both factory made and home-made. The parlor was the shop. Local people could easily call in and take their pick, but there were many farm women in the backwoods who found it difficult to buy a hat unless the hat came to them. My grandmother drove her horse and buggy, with the back crowded with hats, into the dooryard of every farm for ten miles around, and sold the hats that were worn to forty churches. My grandfather was telling me the distances that she had traveled, and the various families to whom she had sold her hats. As usual, it was from him that I could learn about the past. "Oh, my," he said, "she *did* enjoy herself. It was a thing that she looked forward to every year, seeing so many people over again, and learning what had happened in the winter." Suddenly his face changed and I could tell that he had remembered a story. "Did I ever tell you," he said, "about that frame in the sitting room that holds your Grampa Keneston's picture?"

I remembered the picture well. It was the one by which I thought I knew Benjamin Keneston best. His hair and beard were a full white, and his mouth, though it curved down, gave the impression of humor, and fitted my grandfather's stories of him. The frame seemed crude and out of place in the sitting room. I said that I hadn't heard the story.

"One day—I was away somewhere—your grandmother was alone and a gypsy woman came to the door. Now your grandmother doesn't trust gypsies, and of course they are thieves, but this woman looked all right and they had only the one wagon pulled up in front with a fierce-looking man holding the reins, and the woman looked scared, so your grandmother asked her what she had. She had a basket full of picture frames, and your grandmother led her into the kitchen. She laid them all out on the set-tubs. Well, your grandmother liked one right away, the one that's in the sitting room now. She asked how much it was and the gypsy woman said seventy-five cents. It was a lot for a picture frame, but your grandmother had some hats which she hadn't sold and which were seventy-five cents too. So she asked the gypsy woman if she'd like to trade. Well, she looked scared, and said she wouldn't, but there was one hat your grandmother showed her which she really liked. After a while she took it, shaking her head and talking to herself, and packed away all her frames but the one, and ran out to the cart. In about a minute, after the cart had started out, your grandmother heard the man start to shout and swear something terrible, and she heard the woman crying. She went out to the road, but they were already past the sap house and going out of sight. She walked up the road after them just a bit, and do you know what she found? There was the hat she'd traded with the gypsy woman, all torn to pieces and thrown in the gutter."

In a few minutes we were passing the fox farm again, and in another quarter of an hour we waved to Henry on the porch of the store. My grandfather pulled out his watch and said, "We'll be there at ten to twelve, I do believe." The Bradburys' place still looked empty. When we came to the Whittemores', Charlie's chair was sitting on the grass near the road, but Charlie was gone. "Reckon Charlie's gone to bed," said my grandfather. "He finds he has to take naps a good part of the day."

Then we were on the rise, with Aunt Nannie's cottage on our left, and the farmhouse further along on the right. A trace of blue smoke trailed from its chimney. When we started the downgrade, Roger began to trot again, knowing that his stable was close. After we had curved into the yard, I carried the bag of salt into the grain shed while my grandfather backed the carriage into its shelter and unfastened the harness. He led Roger into the barn, past the hayrack, and fetched him grain and a pail of water. "And now," he said to me, catching me by the shoulder, "it's time for our dinner, young man, after a hard morning's work."

My grandmother had the table set by the time we walked in. "Wash your hands," she said. "It's getting cold." When I walked in, the steam was rising from the boiled potatoes. I forked a few and mashed them on my plate, and added two chunks of cold boiled beef and as many fresh peas as I could fit. I sat at one end of the table, while my grandparents faced each other across the middle. They never ate as much as I did, even put together. We all ate slices of baker's bread, and drank glasses of milk, and we finished with coffee and mince pie or sponge cake.

After dinner, we all moved into the living room. My grandfather lay down on the sofa, while my grandmother sat beside him in an overstuffed chair. I sat across the room with a book. Today was one of the days when my grandfather fell asleep. He would sleep for no more than ten minutes, and would often snore like a thunderstorm. Sometimes he would fall asleep with a newspaper over his face, and the paper would flutter and rattle with his breathing.

I put down my book and walked over to the wall to look at the frame with my great-grandfather's picture in it. I touched the workmanship of the rustic finish. Once more I strolled through the gallery of the family, and practiced remembering the names of the people who died before I was born. Suddenly one of my grandfather's eyes cracked open. "What are you prowling around for, boy?" he said quickly. "You might think somebody was asleep."

"Wesley, Wesley," said my grandmother, who refused to admit that anything was a joke.

"How long did I sleep?" he asked.

"Not very 1ong," she said. "At least I don't think so."

He looked at his watch. "Good," he said. "I hope Roger feels as young as I do." He looked at me, smiling. "Boy, how would you like to finish off the Crumbine place today?"

The Crumbine place was a farm which some people from Cleveland used for the summer. It was on the downward slope of Ragged Mountain, off New Canada Road. I remembered when Luigi (a Canuck whose last name I never knew) and Ben Heaton held an auction to sell everything in the house, when they moved out after selling it to the Crumbines. The farm had belonged to the Heatons for generations, and the auctioneer was hawking broken cradles and old quilts and packets of letters: the valueless mementos of generations of farm women. I was six or seven then. The Crumbines tore the house down and built it up again, and planted around it and stuck wagon wheels in the drive until you could have sworn it was a 1935 copy of an old farm, and nothing more.

They wanted the hay cut, and the fields kept trim, and the hay that grew there was very good. So, though it was a long trip to hay it, we did it every summer. From the top of the hayrack, on their high fields, I could see across to the other side of the valley. Sometimes I could even see the Green Mountains of Vermont, pale in the distance. It was always cool up there, and the old Heaton well pumped cold beautiful water, and the long rides with my grandfather were full of stories. I liked to hay there more than anywhere else.

"Can we get it all on?" I said. I was reluctant to have it end.

"We're through with raking," he said. "So we can start right now." I followed him through the kitchen where he put his cap on, and out into the yard toward the barn. "I think we can do three loads before five, and I think we can get it all in three loads. They'll be heavy, but it will be downhill all the way until we get here."

"Okay," I said. I was elated suddenly because it was a test and we could make it a record. "First I've got to feed my chicks."

"Go to," he said, "and I'll harness Roger."

I filled my grain pail and carried it with my water bucket across the road to the chicks. They had finished their morning's grain and dirtied their water. I performed again the process I had followed in the morning. When I came back across the road, the hayrack was emerging from the barn. I was able to set my pails in the grain shed while my grandfather led Roger and turned him around. We climbed into the empty rack and sat on a hard board. My grandfather clucked at Roger, and we creaked down into the yard in front of my grandmother's kitchen door. My grandmother came out on the porch to wave goodbye and we were off again.

We were going toward New Canada, a direction opposite from the direction of the morning. Roger knew what he was pulling and didn't try to trot this time. It was a hot afternoon but when we entered New Canada the sun couldn't reach us. At the sides of the road, which was still washed out in spots from the spring rains, the ferns were bright green in front of the darker brush and pine. Suddenly I thought of something that might start a story. "Did Indians live here?" I asked.

"Yes," he said. "They were a tribe called Pennacooks. Part of the Iroquois, I guess. I don't know much about them, but I expect it's all in books. I've found some arrowheads some days. And a few times I've seen some rock piles that look like those Indian direction-markers. I don't know what became of them."

"Did they fight in the French and Indian wars?"

"I suppose, though I don't rightly know. Of course, folks didn't live up here much until after that, just trappers and some

Frenchmen. Did I ever tell you about your ancestor in that war?"

He had, in fact, but he hadn't told it to me for a long time. "I don't think so," I said. "Tell me."

"He was a soldier and he was fighting the Indians. Uncle Luther might have remembered his name, but I don't. He was off fighting somewhere with the rest of his folks, and they heard that a whole passel of Indians was coming after them, and they decided to get back to their fort. Well, they left their camp, all of them, and went through the forest being very quiet. They got along a good ways and then they remembered that they had left their cooking pot behind them. This was the big iron pot where they cooked their dinner, everything they ate. Somebody had to go get it, so your ancestor said he'd do it. He got back to the old camp and found it, and he started back all right, but then he heard the Indians coming at him from the side. He didn't have time to do much, so he set the pot down beside a stump, top down, hoping they might think it was another stump, I guess, and he crawled inside a hollow log that was lying right across the trail. Well, the Indians stepped right on the hollow log. He felt their moccasins go whack whack over his face and he just lay there and couldn't make a sound though the red ants were stinging him cruelly. When they were all gone he crawled out and took his pot and went home with it. Or so they tell."

We passed the fallen-in jumble which had once been the Godfreys' house and barn, and we passed the new house which Luigi and Ben Heaton had built for themselves after Ben sold the farm to the Crumbines. Old Ben was sitting on the front porch, his great moustaches drooping. He didn't even have the energy to rock his rocking chair. We waved and Ben ponderously nodded.

Half an hour from the house we reached the gate to Crumbine's field. The bars were down, for there were no animals to escape and the Crumbines only kept up their fences for the look of it. The field was open to the sun, and as we rode in, the heat came back on us. But with it came a breeze from the mountains across the valley, and I felt strong. "I'll pitch on," I said.

"You start," said my grandfather. "We can take turns." He

stood up now, and urged Roger across the field to start at the furthest piles. When we came to the first, I plunged my fork into it like a javelin and leapt over the side of the wagon. I was tired soon enough, since I tried to pitch on as quickly as my grandfather. I began to move slowly after half the rack was full, and my grandfather climbed down and announced that it was his turn.

So I mounted the wagon and did the placing and treading. I fell into a rhythm of work so engaging that I didn't notice that we were building a huge load until my grandfather stepped back and said, "I reckon I daren't put on any more, and I reckon that's about right, too."

He climbed up to the front, putting his foot on a shaft. He was sweating, and his dark shirt was darker. He urged Roger toward the gate and New Canada Road. We could see the horse strain forward and shift his weight to get the wheels moving. When we got to the road and turned to start downhill my grandfather said, "Whoa!" and handed me the reins. "Hold tight," he said. "I'm going to fix the drag." Hanging from the rear of the rack by their chains were two flat boards, which he used coming down New Canada with a heavy load of hay. They slid under the rear wheels and prevented them from turning, so that we dragged down the hill instead of rolling. Roger did not have to use all his strength merely to hold the weight back.

As we scraped slowly along the dirt and small stones of New Canada Road, I asked my grandfather if he remembered any more stories about wars. He told me again how his father, John Wells, fought with Grant's army that took Vicksburg. "He stood in line next to Paul Henry Morgan when Paul Henry was killed. Paul Henry was a cousin of your grandmother's people, but of course there wasn't any connection back then. Father had just moved out of the shelter of a big stump, to let Paul Henry take his place, when a great big cannon ball crashed through that stump, and took off Paul Henry's head. Father emptied his pockets and after the war he took the knife and the bits of carving back to the Morgans. The Morgans were people who lived up high on the mountain here. You've seen that ring which Paul Henry carved out of bone and decorated with blood."

"Yes," I said. In fact I used to look at it about twice a day.

"Mighty strange thing for a man to carve, I've always thought." Then he went on to talk aimlessly about his father, the blacksmith with the harelip who debated in the Lyceum. Usually he talked less about his own family than he did about my grandmother's people. I never felt that I knew John Wells as clearly from his stories as I knew Benjamin Keneston.

At the bottom of New Canada Road we stopped again and my grandfather took the drags off. We rolled out onto the flat blacktop and then turned in the drive to pause in front of the kitchen. "Katie!" called my grandfather. "Come see what a load we've fetched."

She came to the door drying her hands on her apron, and clucked and shook her head. "My, my!" she said. "Can Roger get it up to the barn?"

"It's going to take a lot of lugging if he can't," said my grandfather. Then he turned his head to me. "You'd better get down, boy," he said. "We need to save that ton and a half."

I jumped down from the high wagon, jarring my teeth. I stood away from it and decided that it *did* look like the biggest load I had ever seen. The hay was laid out three feet past the rails on each side and it reached so high that I couldn't see over it, even when I stood on the porch.

The hayrack was on level ground in front of the porch, but thirty feet beyond was the short little hill that rose to the barn. My grandfather took the loose rein in his right hand and suddenly whipped it down on Roger's hind quarters. At the same time he shouted at Roger in a most menacing way, and Roger jumped and actually started to run. When he got to the hill he strained and slowed, but he still kept rolling until, with a great leaning effort at the last, he pulled it to the level of the barn and into the dark barn floor.

My grandfather and I pitched off the load before we came down for our coffee. It was hot in the barn, and at first I pitched from the wagon onto the loft while my grandfather fetched Roger a pail of water. I put my shirt on, to keep the chaff from sticking to my body, but I couldn't remember not to breathe, so I paused every few moments to volley several sneezes. When my grandfather climbed up his stout home-made ladder to the loft, he packed away the hay which I had pitched off, and then he jumped down into the wagon to help me lighten the load. When the front edge of the loft was full of hay again, he climbed up and stowed it away. We pitched off our biggest load in less time than we took with an ordinary quantity.

Roger had finished his water. My grandfather backed him out and turned him around, and we let him stand in front of the house while we went inside. I quenched my thirst with well water that my grandmother had drawn, and started on my coffee, but before I could cool it enough to take a sip, my grandfather had finished his. I knew he was in a hurry. I filled my cup to the brim with cold well water, and gulped it down.

"We're off," said my grandfather.

"Now don't hurt yourself with hurrying," said my grandmother.

My grandfather laughed. "Two of us have a long rest between here and the Crumbines'," he said. "Wouldn't say the same for Roger."

We climbed into the wagon and rattled off. Our second load was as big as the first. For a while it looked like a thunderstorm, and we worked fast to get our big load home before it got wet, but when we dragged out of New Canada onto the blacktop, we found sunshine again and a clear sky.

We pitched off as quickly as we had done before, but my back was hurting and I regretted that the thunderstorm had not come. I took a little longer this time with my coffee and I looked forward to the drive, but with dread to the work after the ride. I looked at the kitchen clock just as I finished my coffee. "It's four o'clock," I said.

My grandfather laughed. "You're not thinking of quitting, are you, boy?" I laughed too. "We'll be home for supper a little after five, Katie," he said. "We don't have so much this time, and we'll pitch it off in the morning."

"Why don't you rest," said my grandmother, "and do it in the morning?"

My grandfather shook his head. "In the morning I'll cut the meadow," he said. "And I think it will rain in the night."

On the slow ride up New Canada, we did not say a great deal. Even my grandfather seemed tired, though he was happy at all we had done. The remaining hay was quickly loaded, and it turned out to be smaller than one of our usual rackfuls. My grandfather didn't bother to fix the drag, and we bumped down the long hill quickly. I was sitting beside my grandfather up front, sucking on a piece of grass, when suddenly I heard a great, tinny crash. I looked back and saw the iron rim of one of our wheels bouncing on stones at the side of the road. "The wheel's off!" I shouted.

"No, it's not," my grandfather said. He was laughing. "But a rim fell off all right." He had stopped Roger and we both climbed down. "You get the rim while I fix the drag on the other wheel," he said.

The rim was lying among the ferns at the side of the road. I stood it up, a tall ring of iron from some old forge, and rolled it like a hoop to the wagon. My grandfather had fixed the drag, so that Roger had some help in holding back the load.

"I was afraid of this," my grandfather said. "If we hadn't needed salt this morning, I was a mind to drive the rack down to the pond and soak the wheels. This drought was bound to shrink the wood."

He stood the rim against the wood of the wheel, clearing away pebbles at the bottom so that it lay as close to the wood as it could. He looked around for a large stone, and when he found a good one he tapped the iron rim rapidly, until by fractions of inches the wheel began to slip over the wooden frame again.

"Did I ever tell you about your great-great-great-grandfather?" he said. He leaned up from his work, pausing for breath, and began to snort and laugh. "That was old Mark Bachelor,

Grampa Keneston's mother's grandfather. Grampa Keneston used to tell stories about him that he'd heard from his mother, and they must go back a long ways, to when people first lived here, after the Revolution. One day old Mark was riding a stage when he looked out the window and saw the rear wheel passing them. The whole wheel, not just the rim. They say he flung open the door and jumped out so fast he left his boots inside. The stage turned over, but not with Mark in it."

He had tapped the rim onto the wheel everywhere he could reach. "I'm going to lead Roger a step now," he said. "You tell me when the bottom is on top." Roger dragged the rack forward until I shouted. My grandfather came back and with a few blows fitted the rest of the rim back on.

"There it is," he said. "I suppose we could drive some wedges in, but we're near home and it takes a time to move itself off. Tomorrow we'll soak it in the morning."

He took the drag off the other wheel and we climbed to our seats in front. "We'll be a mite later than I told," he said. He pulled out his watch. "It'll be five-twenty-five before we're home."

I kept looking back but the rim held steady. I was hungry, and happy that we wouldn't be pitching off this load. Beside me I heard my grandfather chuckle. "Did I ever tell you," he said, "about how Mark Bachelor proposed to his wife? I don't know how many times I heard Grampa Keneston tell it. Mark didn't talk much. He knew a girl from church and he used to walk home with her but he never knew what to say. Come time he wanted to marry her, but he didn't know how to ask. He rode up to her one day, when she was in front of her house, and pointed to behind his saddle and said, 'On or off?' "

We both laughed. "I guess she must have climbed up then and there," he said, "or there wouldn't have been any more Bachelors around here."

We drove in the driveway and I jumped down. I watched Roger carry the load easily up to the barn, and I went inside the kitchen. My grandmother was at the stove. "Took you longer than you thought," she said, and I told her what had happened.

That night I ate my favorite sandwich of fried Spam and raw onions, and had a Pepsi-Cola with it instead of milk. After supper, while my grandfather milked, I lay down on my bed for half an hour and rested, reading a paper-backed collection of short stories. I went up to the tie-up just as he was finishing, and helped him clean it. Then we walked arm in arm down to the house, and sat reading in the living room. I was sleepy, and yawned between sentences. At nine o'clock Gabriel Heatter told us that the skies of Europe were black with young Americans, massively bombing Germany. At a quarter past, assured that everything was both momentous and bound to turn out all right, we turned off the radio, ate our snacks, and went to bed.

At two o'clock I woke up and was fully awake with a sudden fright. I had not remembered to shut up my chickens. I tiptoed out through my grandparents' room, hearing their even old breathing, and unlocked the door. The moon was bright. I hurt my feet on the stones of the driveway. And when I had crossed the smooth road I stumbled over the roots and bushes in the hen yard, on the way to my chickens. In my mind's eye I could see the carnage of two hundred chicks.

But they were safe. As I came up to their open pen, something seemed to move off in the heavy grass, but it might have been only my fear. I picked off the two chicks that roosted on a bush and deposited them with the rest in their little cage, and I fixed the catch on the door. I walked back to the house and my bed, thinking how lucky it was that the fox in the barn had not been alive tonight.

EIGHT

THE BLUEBERRY PICKING

O NE DAY in late July 1945, I woke at six when my grandmother brought the black coffee into my bedroom. I sat on the edge of the bed and gulped it down. It was made in an old drip coffee pot on the iron stove, where a kettle was always simmering, and it was nearly as thick as Turkish. The shades were still down, and the morning light showed in a thousand pinpricks through the worn green cloth. I crossed the room and opened the shades, and heard a rooster crow in the hen yard across the road. A big automobile blew past, making an early start for the White Mountains. I always looked out to see what kind of day it would be. Rain? A scorcher? It looked fine and sunny today. I walked back to the bed, where my coffee cup sat on the table between my typewriter and a vase of flowers which my grandmother had picked. I sat on the bright quilt and finished the coffee.

This was the start of a day we had planned for weeks. In the years past, before I was born, my grandfather had made an annual excursion to pick blueberries. I had heard about those days in many of his stories. The blueberries were the low, wild kind, and they grew among the ledges of blue rock at the top of Ragged Mountain. They were a three-mile walk from the farmhouse, and the walk was mostly up. When my grandfather was younger, he and a hired man would pick for one long day, and my grandmother and her daughters would wash, sort, and can them for two days. A shelf of cold-packed quarts of blueberries would wait in the cellar for the piecrusts of winter. It was one of the many ways in which a farmer compensated for his lack of cash-like the eggs from the laying season stored in waterglass, and like the salted meat from the slaughtering.

My grandfather had talked about it so much that it seemed as much past as the Lyceum and the two-hour sermons. But a few weeks earlier, this past had strangely seemed present to us. Paul Whittier had been chasing a bear which had tramped down his peas, and had followed him all the way to the top of Ragged. (It was not only a lust for revenge which drove him; the anachronistic bounty on bears was $50.) He had lost his bear among the rocks on the other side of the mountain, but among the blue ledges of the top he had found the blueberries thicker than ever. They were green then, or he said he would have been up there eating them still.

No one, as far as my grandfather knew, had picked there for twenty years. The berries were higher up than the forests which had been cut of their soft wood ten years before, or the lumberjacks would have stripped them. No one else in the neighborhood would have cared to make the climb. The thought of all those blueberry pies growing, maturing, and dropping every year—unappreciated except by the birds—troubled my grandfather's sense of propriety. We decided we would go blueberry picking that year.

My grandmother fretted a little: it was a long trip; the rocks were hard to climb; the blueberries would be too heavy for us to carry; my grandfather was too old. But the thought of her rows of blueberries, cold-packed in their quart jars, overcame her opposition. She made us promise to stop and rest when we were tired, and my grandfather fixed the time when he thought the blueberries would be ripe.

This morning I took my second cup of coffee in the kitchen, and ate breakfast in the old chair beside the window, under the canary named Christopher. I was impatient to be started. I heard a strange noise outside, a high-pitched hoot from behind the sheep barn, where railroad tracks of the Boston and Maine cut through the soft dirt. It was the time for the morning Peanut, the train that went up to White River Junction in the evening and came back in the morning, but the whistle of the Peanut was the long, throaty lament of the steam engine. I stared at the gap in the ensilage corn through which I would be able to see the train flash. When it came it looked like a trolley car, short and self-propelled, and it hooted again its ridiculous horn. "I suppose that's one of these new Diesels," my grandmother said. "Somebody said they'd seen one this summer."

When I had finished my eggs, I walked up to the tie-up where my grandfather was doing the morning chores. The cows were moving out to pasture, and behind them my grandfather was clapping his hands and shouting. In the spring they would gallop out like young horses, but by this time of year they acted like cows again, and my grandfather was in a hurry to shut the gates behind them. I went into the tie-up to start cleaning it. With the edge of a hoe I lifted up the hinged floorboard over the manure pit, and splattered the cowflops onto their cousins below. My grandfather came in. "How did you like the new whistle?" he said.

"Not so much," I told him. "I like the old kind."

"I suppose there's a reason for it," he said. He picked up the other hoe and scraped along with me. "You should be resting," he said, "for what's ahead of you." He sang one of his tuneless songs, and seemed as excited as I was.

When we walked into the kitchen, my grandmother was packing pie and sandwiches into an enormous paper bag. "You'll need your strength," she said. "Now, Wesley, you eat a good breakfast." He ate his oatmeal and bread and coffee, sitting at one of the set-tubs which was covered with oilcloth. My grandmother finished packing the paper bag and disappeared into the shed. A moment later I heard her pumping at the deep well in the back, and I followed her out to relieve her. I pumped and we filled three milk bottles with cold well water, and she put cardboard tops on the bottles.

We left them inside the shed, and brought the paper bag out with us when my grandfather had finished eating. Two huge pails, shaped wider at the bottom than at the top, lay waiting for us. We put the food in one and the water in the other. Then my grandfather found a wooden yoke which went over the back of his neck, from which the two great pails hung down like enormous earrings. It was the apparatus he used when he made maple sugar in the winter, pouring the sap from the little buckets at each sugar maple into the big pails. I carried two sap buckets in which we would pick the berries, and we started off.

It was seven o'clock. The air was cool and the grass was soaking wet under our feet. Low light from the east came through the trees, which were full and dark green. My grandmother called after us from the end of the porch, warning us to be careful. We turned into New Canada Road and started to climb. "It'll be heavy coming back," said my grandfather, "but at least it will be downhill." He paused, the light buckets swinging easily from the ends of the yoke. Then he laughed. "The only man I ever knew," he said, "who could walk all day and not be tired was your GreatGrampa Keneston. He must have touched every inch of this mountain. Days when he couldn't do much else he would walk around his pasture looking at the fencing. My, he was sprightly. You heard your mother tell about how, the day before he died, he walked clear down to West Andover to buy some Canada Mints. He was eighty-seven then. When he had his seventieth birthday, he stood up on the horse's back and galloped up the hill to the barn. Bethuel Peasley told how when he was seventy-five or so he set off on a walk with a two-year-old dog following him, and he came back four hours later with the dog slung along the back of his neck like a lamb. All tired out."

In the shade of the gray birch, and of the maples that met over New Canada Road, it was almost cold that morning, but I was already sweating because of the climb. I took off the sweater which my grandmother had asked me to wear and tied it around my waist. "That's the last you'll use your sweater today," my grandfather said.

After a mile of New Canada Road, we climbed over some bars into a pasture. I thought I felt ruts underneath the old leaves where we were walking. "Is this a lumber road?" I asked.

"Yes," said my grandfather. "It's Paul Whittier's pasture,

though he only keeps a few head now. He took the lumber off about ten years ago." The only old trees were twisted ones which the lumberers had scorned. Young fir was growing thickly everywhere but the road, which the spring waters had eroded into cliffs and islands of rock. I fell and scraped my knee. We climbed most of the time, but the road avoided the steepest parts. Sometimes we passed through a clearing, flatter than the rest of the land, which the cows patronized. Squashed bushes grew there among the cowflops: new and steaming, old and gray.

At a little after eight, we paused in one of those clearings and sat on rocks to catch our breath. My grandfather's shirt was wet through. I already felt as tired as if I had hayed for a whole afternoon. We said nothing for a while. Then I said, "I'm thirsty."

My grandfather shook his head. "You'll be thirstier," he said. "It's thirsty work. You'll do better to wait."

In a moment we set out again. The road failed us and we climbed a stone wall out of Paul Whittier's pasture. "I reckon this is part of our land you've never seen," said my grandfather. "Took the timber off nearly twenty years ago." Pine grew tall around us. "It won't be long before we take it off again."

We walked parallel to the stone wall until we came to a dry creek bed, and we used it as our road up the mountain. It was very rocky and I found myself using my hands to climb with. "How will we get down," I asked, "when we're carrying blueberries?"

"There are other ways," said my grandfather. We stood still for a moment in order to talk. "Or there used to be. One way is steeper than most of this but it's steadier. Not that this creek used to be so dug out. I suppose you can't know what you will find." We both wiped our faces with our handkerchiefs. I looked at my watch and it was only eight-thirty. "We'd better move on," my grandfather said.

After fifteen minutes of climbing, we left the creek and came to more level land. A surprising plain of heavy grass made easy walking for a moment. "Too bad we can't get the hayrack up here," I said. My grandfather nodded and smiled. He was looking ahead at the fringe of trees on the edge of the clearing. When we came up to them, he motioned to me to go first. I stepped through and stopped still. The land in front of me sloped slightly, and I saw that it raised again two hundred yards further, making a little saucer of a valley high up on the mountain. In the bowl, flat down and rust red, and all pointing in the same direction, lay a forest of dead trees.

It could not have been larger than ten acres, but it seemed vast as I looked at it, like a crater of the dead. Desolation made it look immense. There seemed to be no growth under the dead branches of the huge trees. The soil had fallen away from the exposed roots, and the roots looked like bunches of dead nerves. We were so high, beyond paths and people, that it seemed as if we were the first to know. I felt as if I had been walking on the shore and found a drowned submarine rolled up by the tide.

My grandfather was looking over my shoulder. "The hurricane?" I asked. I meant the storm of September 1938.

"Yes," said my grandfather. "Do you know what kind of trees they were?"

I shook my head.

"This was the stand of rock maple," he said. "It must have taken a hundred and fifty years to grow so big. They would have been worth hauling from here, being rock maple." The chopping block in the woodshed was rock maple, I knew. It was about the hardest wood which grew in New England. "We were planning to sell them in 1940 but after everything blew down nobody would come up here for them. They were too busy with the trees low down."

I had nothing to say. I just stared. It was so huge and so wasted.

"Dead but not buried," my grandfather went on. "I hadn't seen it since the time I climbed up here after the hurricane. Pine a few rods away wasn't touched. The roots aren't deep here; that's why I feared and climbed up. There's ledge down a few feet. It looked different then. You couldn't see the trunks for all the leaves, and of course you couldn't walk through it. I could see that everything was pointing the same way. A lumber man from the government told me one gust probably did it."

A moment later my grandfather stepped past me and we began to pick our way through the dead trees. The branches made a continuous dry hedge which snapped at the touch and scratched our faces and arms. My watch was nearly torn from my wrist. I put it in my pocket. We climbed over and under the great trunks, and weaved back and forth as if we were lost in a maze. Finally we rose at the other side of the lot, and looked back again. "We won't be coming through here on the way back," said my grandfather. "Lucky thing." He took one last look at his trees and then turned up the hill.

We were beginning to climb the blue ledges which made the top of Ragged. It was only four hundred yards to the blueberries, but they were hard going. "I can see the bushes," said my grandfather. My feet felt lighter and I climbed more rapidly. Only my throat remained tight and dry, and I looked forward to water as much as to sitting down. Soon the dome of Ragged flattened out, and the rocks which had seemed to lie closely together turned into islands in a sea of blueberries.

They were as low as grass, hardly taller than the flat rock they surrounded. The blue of the berries seemed more prominent than the green of the leaves, so that the earth looked blue everywhere—from blue stone to blue fruit. Only the texture varied. The berries were ripe and full. Some of them had burst and oozed a blue liquid. Most of them were small, and as sweet as I had ever tasted.

We squatted on a rock. My grandfather delved into his pails. "Now's when the work starts," he said, "so I reckon you'll want some strength." He opened the paper bag and handed me a sandwich. I looked at my watch and it was nine o' clock. "Have yourself some water," he said.

The milk bottle of well water was already warm. I pried the top off and tilted my head back and swallowed luxuriously. When I took it away, I had drunk nearly half the bottle. My grandfather looked over. "Careful," he said. "It's a hot day and a long way to water."

I nodded but I didn't really care. I took another sip before

I put it back. Then I ate my egg sandwich while the sun rose higher and warmed the back of my neck. There was no wind this morning, or we would have been open to it. I realized that we had left trees behind at the level of the dead forest. I looked down at it now, a red-brown patch among the green. Elsewhere, as far as I could see, there was only the green of the trees and the blue-silver of small lakes. Here and there in the distance I saw the white of a farmhouse. Suddenly something occurred to me. "I should think that rock maple might catch on fire," I said.

My grandfather nodded. "Lightning might do it," he said. "Of course nobody walks up here to throw a cigarette away. I've thought of it. It would blaze down the whole mountain if it started, and we're on the mountain."

I stood up and walked a little way toward the other side of Ragged. I felt as solitary as an explorer. A low cloud stopped another peak a few miles off, and in between I saw the same green, and the same white specks of the farms.

I heard my grandfather call, "Want any more to eat now?" He was packing up the lunch.

"I guess not," I said, and walked back next to him. He put the bag and the bottles in a crack in the rock, and stood up.

"All set?" he said. He handed me one of the sap buckets. The two big pails were standing on a flat piece of rock. "These berries are mighty low," he said. "You may prefer to sit on the rock and pick them. A sore back is a sore back."

We each took a pail and set out in different directions. I had never picked low-bush berries before, and there were tricks I didn't know. When I tried to scoop off a handful at once, I crushed some of the berries and pulled a leaf or a bit of stem along with them. My pail was full of foreign matter, which would make for a lot of picking over back at the farm. Yet when I tried to be careful I went so slowly that it would have taken all morning to pick one bucket. The trouble with sitting was that I had to slide myself over the bumpy rock, and I began to feel paralyzed where I sat. The heaviest stems of berries were always slightly out of reach. I tried kneeling, but my knees gave out. I tried standing, and it felt all right until I unbent, when I thought I would crack apart. Finally I sat again, as the least evil.

My grandfather stood and bent. Whenever he straightened up he grimaced. "Why don't *you* sit down?" I asked.

"I'd never stand up again!" he said. He pointed to the calves of his legs without breaking the rhythm of his fast picking. "Cramps," he said. "From climbing up here."

I picked and picked. I switched from the right hand to the left and back again and picked two-handed, and still my pail was only a quarter full. I realized that even when I had filled it, it would barely cover the bottom of one of the big pails. I thought we would never fill even one of them. Then I heard my grandfather grunt as he straightened up, and saw him empty his full bucket into one of the big pails. "There's one," he said.

"Look at all I've done," I said, lifting my pail to show it to him.

"You don't know how to pick them yet." He walked over to me and leaned down. He took hold of a stem heavy with blueberries and stripped it clean between his index and middle fingers, without crushing a berry or tearing off a leaf. "Do you see?" he said. "You have to be gentle and let your hand feel them coming. You'll learn it."

In the whole morning I only filled my pail twice, while his pail emptied itself five times into our storage bins on the flat rock. My hands felt twisted out of shape and nervous with their continual darting. My back felt welded in a leaning curve. Worst of all, my throat parched with the thirst, and parched more and more as the sun rose in the sky and the sweat dried on my body. A hundred times I almost complained, or almost rose to have a drink of the water without saying anything, but each time the sight of my grandfather—picking steadily and humming to himself, and seventy-two years old—shamed me into silence. He worked with utter delight in the growing pile of berries. He talked of the number of blueberry pies which we had already gathered, and all I could think of was the dampness of them. When I ate a handful of blueberries, my mouth felt better for a moment, but then felt unutterably worse: so thick that its sides would stick together, and my tongue clung to the roof of my mouth. I knew that we would break for lunch, but I had put my watch in my pocket. I kept squinting up at the sun to guess the time. Finally, when I didn't even know I was going to say it, I heard my dry voice squeaking, "I think I'll have a drink."

My grandfather pulled his gold watch from the pocket of his trousers. "My, my," he said. "It's past lunch time. Twelve-fifteen." He put his watch away and stretched carefully. "I guess we'd better do some eating."

I rose gratefully and walked toward our cache of food and water. I lifted the bottle I had started before and, though I knew I was foolish, drained it dry. A minute after I had set it back on the rock, my thirst returned. I reached for a second quart, which stood propped against rock in the crack, and when I lifted it out my stiff fingers slipped, and the bottle fell and rolled from me, and the water poured out over the blue rocks and drained among the blueberry plants. "Look!" I said. I was exhausted and angry to the point of tears. I could say nothing more.

My grandfather shook his head and smiled at me. "I suspect you'll wish you had that quart of water," he said. I dipped my finger in a small puddle in the rock and sucked it. The third quart had to do for both of us now, and my grandfather hadn't drunk anything yet.

"You handle the other quart," I said.

"We'll be careful with that one."

As I ate, I felt a little better. The custard pie, the pickles, and the butter in the chicken sandwiches were all damp. I ate as slowly as I could, pushing away the moment when the picking began again. When we had finished the whole bag, my grandfather tucked it tidily—waxed paper and hard-boiled-egg shells inside—into a crevice of the stone.

"Now let's have a bit of that water," said my grandfather. He lifted the remaining bottle and took a mouthful, keeping it in his mouth a long time, and letting it go down in slow sips, luxuriously. "That's good," he said, and handed it to me. I tried to do the same trick, and choked.

He stood up and stretched again. "I could relish a few minutes on the sofa just now," he said. "Don't see any sofas hereabouts." He walked to where he had left his pail, and began to pick again.

I looked at my watch. It was nearly one o'clock. On my way to my bucket, I looked in the big pails. One was nearly full, and the other was barely covered with berries on the bottom. When I sat down on the hard rock again, my old bruises of the morning felt worse than before, and I suppose I felt more tired than I did three hours later.

During the afternoon I filled my bucket more rapidly, and every time I emptied it I took a sip of water. It was my reward for being quick. I saw my grandfather wet his lips once, and stand staring across the valley below us at the hills on the other side. I stood up and watched with him, and for a moment forgot blueberries and sore backs, fatigue and thirst. But in a moment my throat contracted with its drought again, and I raced to fill up another pail.

My grandfather seemed to pick more slowly than he had picked in the morning, and when he stood up to carry the bucket to the big pail, he usually paused for a minute before walking. In the middle of the afternoon I calculated that two more bucketfuls would fill the last big pail, and I raced to fill my bucket and be done. My grandfather and I met at the big pails at the same time, and poured our blueberries to the very top. I took another sip of water, unable to speak with the dryness of my throat. About an inch was left in the bottom of the bottle. I was already thinking of the well water at home, after our walk down the mountain, but then I saw my grandfather walk back to the berries.

"What are you doing?" I said. "We filled the pails."

"Not these," he said, waving the sap bucket. "Are you tired?" He set the bucket down and walked back to where I was standing. "I didn't think of that."

"No," I said.

"We could go home," he said. "We have plenty of berries."

"No, no," I said. "I don't want to."

I would have been ecstatic if he had overruled me, but he didn't. He said, "You really sure?" and when I nodded he walked back to his berries. When he turned away, I was filled with anger and frustration, and I lifted the milk bottle and drained the last of the water.

We each filled our buckets. My grandfather was finished a moment before me, and he gathered a few handfuls to top off mine. We carried the sap buckets to the high rock where the two big pails stood. We looked all around us once more. It was only threethirty, but a wind was rising and I began to feel a little cool. My grandfather put the milk bottles in the pockets of his overalls. He fastened the ends of the wooden yoke to the two big pails and lifted them. His face looked red, and veins stood out on his temples. "It must be very heavy," I said. I lifted the sap buckets and they were heavy enough to suit me.

"They're tolerably heavy," he said, and started along the stones.

"Let me carry them," I said rather feebly. I didn't even hear his answer, and he kept walking straight on.

As I walked my thirst seemed to grow and grow, until I found it utterly intolerable. We were going slowly down a steep grassy slope. If there had been a cliff handy, I would have been tempted to jump from it. I felt as if my throat were being stung by red ants. My lips felt as if they were cracking open, and my tongue felt as dry as old newspaper. "Is there any water on the way?" I asked when I came abreast of my grandfather.

We had been walking for ten minutes. When my grandfather turned to me, his face was dead white. I was shocked. He knelt until the pails touched the ground and then shrugged from under the yoke. He sat on the ground and I thought he was going to be sick. "Might be," he said.

"Are you all right?" I asked

"Don't worry," he said. "Don't worry." His face gradually relaxed and color returned to his cheeks.

"It's my turn to carry the yoke," I said. "My hands hurt from the wire handles of these buckets, and anyway, I want to learn how to carry the yoke."

He looked at me. "It's a longer walk if we go by water. Are
you that thirsty?"

"I am thirsty, but I want to carry."

"All right," he said, "you young bull." I didn't feel much like a
bull. "I guess I shouldn't be surprised. See if you like it."

The novelty of the yoke took my mind off my thirst. When
I crouched under it and stood up, I nearly lost my balance. I
swayed with the pails dangling clumsily at my sides. Then I
hunched forward and they settled. My grandfather picked up
the sap buckets and looked at me. "All right?" he said.

"I guess so," I said. "Go slowly."

We doubled back a few yards and then started to walk north
on the same level, moving away from the farmhouse. At first I
had to walk very cautiously, because the rhythm of the swinging pails threatened my balance, but soon I learned to use the
swing of the weight to help me keep moving, and I shrugged
until the yoke felt comfortable on the back of my neck. When I
felt secure in the walking, the thirst came back upon me.

After a few minutes my grandfather felt able to talk again. I
realized that today had been the most silent day we had ever
spent together, and I decided that he must have been more tired
than I had suspected all along. "I had that pain in my side," he
said, "which comes when I run sometimes. I'd rather you didn't
say much about it back home. Katie frets so much." I said I
wouldn't. "I'm glad to show you the pool where we'll find the
water, if it's still there. It was there six years ago. No, eight years.
It was there

about eighty years ago, for that matter. But on the way I'm
going to show you something else."

"What is it?"

"You wait," he said. "Seeing will be good enough for you."
Then he snorted and remembered an anecdote about a man
from Concord who was curious about how Lucas Blount had
lost his leg, and how Lucas Blount left him more curious than
ever. He seemed himself again.

We had passed the forest of dead rock maples, going slightly

below it, and then we had followed a steep path downhill for
several hundred yards. Now we came on to a part of Ragged
which was entirely new to me. It seemed to be a high plain, quite
level and thick with fir trees. Ragged could hardly be called a
mountain, or even a hill, any longer. Then we descended a few
feet into what looked like a narrow, flat road. I saw that banks
rose on either side of it, perhaps twelve feet apart. It was too
level for one of the makeshift lumber roads. Branches leaned together over it, but only goldenrod and small bushes were growing in its narrow path. "What's this?" I asked, as I paused when
I had scrambled down to it.

"Look," said my grandfather, and pointed to the ground. First
I was aware that the path seemed made of ridges going from
side to side, like a corduroy road except that the ridges were a
foot apart. Then I saw what looked like long streaks of orange,
running parallel across the ends of the ridges.

"It's a railroad!" I said.

"It used to be," he said. "I remember when they closed it down.
It's narrow gauge, see? One of your Foster cousins was a brake-
man here. It was just a little branch line, built for hauling timber
to the freight depots. They took the mail and some passengers
too, when there were any, when there were more people here."

We walked on the rotted ties. Except that we had to duck
overhanging branches, it was the easiest walking of the day.
Here and there one of the banks had caved in, and dirt had fall-
en onto the old track, but most of it seemed nearly intact. It was
like Pompeii, and the close foliage of the heavy trees around us
closed us in, as if we were sealed off in an alley separate from the
world of Diesels.

"Where did it go?" I asked.

"It stopped just back there, at no place. They called it Ragged Station. Nothing's there now but I'll show you where it
was sometime. Wash used the wood from the old station when
he built his lean-to. Up here is where your Great-Grampa Keneston came from, you know."

I had the pails working well now, and took giant steps, two

ties at a time. We walked in silence for a way. I was watching the ties as I walked and seldom looked up. To slip and fall would have meant blueberry picking all over again, and the very thought of it made the fire in my throat sizzle. Then I heard my grandfather say, "Hold on there, boy. Look ahead."

He stood out of my way. Ahead was something dark and covered with vines. It obstructed the tracks we walked on. My grandfather stopped. I set down the yoke and the blueberries and walked past him. Under the wooden hulk of the coal car the red wheels fitted the red tracks. I could see fungi growing on the rotten sides where the vines were thinnest. Then I looked beyond the coal car to the red, pitted hulk of the locomotive. As I started to edge my way toward it, I looked back and saw my grandfather follow, grinning in his delight at my excitement.

Branches leaned in the cab, where the throttle, corroded with rust, stood out from the rusted instruments. The coal shovel lay in the bottom of the cab, and, though leaves had drifted into every opening, I could see that there was still a heap of coal in the coal car. I walked around the engine. It was intact, down to the rope which led to the bell dangling in front. The smokestack was tall, and the unbroken glass of the headlight covered an oil lamp. The apparatus of wheels and pistons was fixed in a red trance, yet it looked as perfect as if it had just moved to a stop. Nothing had come loose or fallen. I had a momentary vision that my grandfather and I would clean the boiler, carry water, light a fire, heap on coal, blow the whistle, and gradually pull the throttle toward us; I saw the old pistons groan and start to move, flecks of rust fall like red snow from the whole machine, and the wheels turn on the red tracks as we plunged ahead on the dead railway, going nowhere on an errand among the farms of the past.

"Why did they leave it here?" I said.

"Nobody ever said. I suppose because of the gauge. It would be hard work moving it anywhere anybody could use it, even for scrap." He was grinning at me. "Now I bet you feel like an explorer," he said.

I didn't want to tell him what I had been thinking. I came back to the cab with the idea of getting up into it, but when I set my foot on the rung outside, it broke off.

"I wonder how long it will stay here," I said.

"Shouldn't wonder if it kept up a hundred years," he said. "It's been here for fifty now."

We walked back along the coal car. I knocked off some of the fungi and saw the black paint blistered underneath. My grandfather walked ahead of me, and lifted the yoke and straightened his shoulders under it. "You ready?" he said. "You've got more to see before you're home again."

"You let me do that," I said.

"I'll carry it to the water," he said. "You fetch the buckets." He started off. I walked after him, edging past the locomotive, and my neck began to straighten itself from the posture it had learned under the yoke. But as soon as we were well past the engine, my thirst returned.

We continued on the track for only two hundred yards. Then my grandfather turned and squatted so that the big pails rested on the ground and relieved him of their weight. "Here's where we go off," he said. "First you walk up ahead fifty yards and take a look. Leave your buckets. Be careful when you get up there."

My thirst had returned so badly that any delay was agony, but I did what he said. The foliage leaned over the track thickly and I couldn't see far ahead. I trotted lightly in order to be done quicker. Then suddenly the foliage thinned and I saw the track go on ahead of me in mid-air. Below was a ravine, cut by the tiny stream I could see at the bottom. It was spanned by a rotting trestle which had mostly fallen away, but across which the red rails narrowly tottered still. I took one long look. This is where my grandfather and I would have driven my imagined train. Then I turned and trotted back to my grandfather.

When he saw me coming, he stood up under the yoke again. I saw the veins stand out at his temples. I picked up my buckets. "Is it standing?" he said. I told him. "When they built it," he said, "they said it would last. Washington helped to keep it up, when he was a young man."

We turned from the track into the forest and immediately started to go downhill. The growth was thick and my grandfather moved slowly with the yoke.

"Are you all right, carrying that?" I asked.

"We're pretty close," he said. Soon we came into a pine forest. The trees were tall and as straight as the masts of ships. It was like walking under water, the way the light moved down through the green needles. Only a few low branches bothered our walking, and they snapped off when we brushed them. The needles felt as soft as air underneath my hot feet. I would have enjoyed it if the thirst had not throbbed in my mouth and throat.

I wanted to talk just to forget the hurt. "Is this virgin pine?" I asked. The moment I asked it, I knew it was a stupid question.

My grandfather laughed. He started to say something, but he was out of breath. "I'll tell you later," he said in gasps.

In a few minutes we left the pine and entered a clearing where I could see only a few ancient maples and some bushes. He set the pails on the ground and ducked out of the yoke. I could see by his face that he had the pain again. I set my buckets beside the pails. "It's my turn now," I said.

He gestured down a slope at one side of the clearing. "Water down there," he said.

I jogged down the slope and found a pool at the bottom. I dropped to my knees and cupped the water in my hands and splashed it into my mouth. The first water seemed painful because it was so meager. I brought more and more upward to my mouth, and covered my shirt with the drips from my fingers. Finally I sat back panting to wait for a second wind. Then my grandfather came walking down the slope beside me, and took a quart bottle from his pocket and filled it and drank from it.

I borrowed it for my second round of drinking, and in a few minutes stood up, my stomach cramped full of water. My grandfather filled the quart again and put the cardboard stopper on it. "For the trip home," he said. He looked better now.

I looked at the pool for the first time. It was small and perfectly round. It looked utterly still, yet the water was clear and cool, with no scum on top and only a few lily pads to vary the surface.

My grandfather saw me looking at it. "God's pool," he said. "Uncle Luther used to walk up here, summers when he took a vacation from Connecticut, back when he was young enough, back before he retired. I believe he used to read books here, or write sermons maybe. I was afraid it might not be here any more. You never can be sure. A stream can shift underground. It comes from the stream which you saw under the trestle, and it goes out beneath that tree. I suppose it's one of the streams which fills up our lake down below."

"It's good water," I said. "I remember Uncle Luther telling me about it."

"In the old days, before they had a well, lots of your ancestors drew all their water here. Come back up and I'll show you something."

"How do you feel?" I asked.

"Better," he said. "Come along."

I followed him back to the clearing with the maples. He pointed with his foot to a flat stone. "Many people of your blood stepped on that stone," he said. "That's the doorstep, and there's the cellar hole." I looked behind the stone and saw the depression in the ground, a small cellar hole walled with dry stone, where the potatoes and apples and carrots and turnips and cabbages and parsnips and salted meat and fish had been stored for decades of winter. "Is this ... ?" I began.

"The Kenestons," he said. "Uncle Luther grew up here, and your Great-Grampa Benjamin, and the others before him. The well they dug is over that way, so mind your feet when you look around. They tapped the stream that flowed from the pool when they got tired of hauling it up that slope in buckets."

I wandered in the old dooryard. A maple above me stretched out a great branch which must have suspended a swing for the children. I stubbed my toe on an old piece of metal that stuck up through the ground. It was the wheel of a cultivator.

My grandfather sat on the doorstep. "I'm sorry to stop," he said. "I know you'd like some coffee and pie. I didn't reckon I'd get so tired." He paused a moment, looking at his hands. "You know the timber you asked about? You thought it might be virgin pine?" he said. "Your great-grandfather cut the virgin timber there, in the fifties, before the war. He stumped it with oxen and planted it with potatoes and hired a crew to dig them in the fall and he hauled them to the old railroad and sold them to a man who took them clear down to Boston, to sell them in the big vegetable market down there. But when the war came he couldn't hire a crew, and the fields grew up with bush, and after the war he just couldn't get started again. He lived so long he sold the pine twice, from the land he cleared and stumped himself I reckon to sell it the third time, come next spring."

I wandered to the other side of the clearing, into a bushy meadow which slanted steeply downward. Under my feet I felt the earth wave like the sea, and I suddenly realized that I was walking on land which retained the ridges which my great-grandfather had plowed into it. I came back to my grandfather. He was examining his hands again and did not hear me coming. I saw how old his hands looked. Then he looked over at the yoke. "Do you really feel like carrying that?" he asked.

"Sure I do," I said. I took a swallow of water and then lifted the yoke again, and settled it where I liked it on my neck. My grandfather lifted the sap buckets and led the way. We descended the bushy meadow into a strip of forest, and then climbed an old stone wall to a road.

My grandfather laughed. "You know where we are?" he asked. "New Canada?" I said hopefully.

"Almost," he said. "Two hundred yards down we come to New Canada. This is what they called New Road, and the town keeps it up though I don't know as anybody's living on it now." We turned into New Canada and walked downhill all the way home. It was four miles, and my back was sore, but my strength revived when I imagined coffee and pie waiting on the oilcloth of the set-tubs. We walked quietly past Washington Woodward's camp, for fear he could discover us and want to chat for an hour or two; he was too lame to walk with us any more.

At last we turned onto the macadam of the main road, and in a moment I saw the white smoke of our chimney. "Well," I said with sudden gaiety, "we've brought the berries."

"Yes," said my grandfather, "and I don't know when we'll make the trip again. I'm glad I could show you some things to remember."

NINE

OLD HOME

THE SUMMER I was seventeen, I kept a racing bike at the farm. The handles turned down and the seat stuck up, and I could make it go very fast. I raced down to Henry Powers's store on the blacktop, and ate a Dr. I.Q., and pedaled over to Mrs. Fortune's for the mail. Henry couldn't keep the post office any more because he had reached the retirement age for postmasters.

One morning when I was biking to the post office Ted Currier came up behind me in his car. I sprinted as hard as I could and kept up with him for a few yards. Then he stepped on the gas and passed me, and, just as I was struggling to go even faster, my left foot slipped off the metal pedal, where I had cut off the leather straps which would have held my toes. I skidded on my side for twenty feet. The front wheel of my bicycle was bent, and the skin was rubbed off my left side. At first an arm and rib cage felt numb. I caught my breath and picked some of the tatters of my shirt out of my wound. Then I lifted my bent bike under my right arm and walked the three-quarters of a mile back to the farm. The Bradburys' place seemed empty. I guessed that Hester had driven from Franklin to take her old parents out for a ride. No one was outside at the Whittemores', and I didn't want to bother Charlie.

At home my grandmother responded to the crisis by being efficient. "Wesley!" she shouted out the window, and began immediately to pull away the remainder of my tee-shirt from my bloody side.

My grandfather clumped through the shed and into the kitchen without stopping to take off his boots. He took a quick look at my shoulder and side. "Anything broken?"

"No," I said. It was beginning to hurt. I told them what had happened.

"Should I call Dr. Clough?" said my grandfather.

"No," said my grandmother. "Fetch me the Rawleigh's Salve." It was exactly the sentence I would have predicted if I had thought about it. Rawleigh's Salve was one of Washington Woodward's contributions to the family. He had peddled it, along with Quaker Oil and his other patent medicines, and none of his customers were more delighted than his family. Rawleigh's cured boils and cuts and sores and burns—for man and beast. I've seen it poultice a cow and turn an aunt's sunburn into a tan. My grandmother spread it gently on the torn flesh, and put gauze on top of it, and secured the gauze with adhesive tape.

For a week, I moved as if I were built of match-sticks and not very much glue. But after three days the salve seemed already to be turning into skin, and after ten days I was haying again. Yet the week of convalescence was a pleasure too. That summer I enjoyed the haying less than I had before. Going fast on my bike was what I really liked. I loved the old people still, but I missed some of the people I knew at school. It was the first time that I had ever felt lonely on the farm.

One morning when I was nearly better, I was sitting on the porch with a book. My grandmother was making pies and my grandfather was fixing the mowing machine. In the distance I saw Mary Bradbury walking down the blacktop from the hill which separated our two houses. She never walked to see us— she never socialized with anybody, except at church—and I was curious.

"Hi," I said.

She looked at me but didn't answer. She looked nervous and I noticed that she was wearing her apron. "Where's Kate?" she said, and then she stood in front of the house and cried, "Katie!"

My grandmother bustled out of the kitchen, slapping her hands and making a little cloud of flour. "Mary," she said.

"William's dead," said Mary. "Can I use the phone?"

My grandmother put her arm around Mary, and took her into the kitchen. I could hear them talking. "He went to bed like he always did. I didn't notice anything. Because of the way he snored I slept in the front room, you know. I got up and laid the fire and he didn't say anything so I figured I would let him sleep. Then I went in when I'd had my breakfast, and he was cold."

My grandmother rang up central and asked for a number in Franklin. "That you, Hester?" she said, in a voice which tried to conceal its feeling. "Here's your mother," and I heard Mary telling Hester.

All morning long it went on. They told other relatives, and they sent a telegram to the son at his Army base in Virginia. They called the undertaker and the minister, and they settled the time of the funeral. My grandmother walked back to the Bradburys' house with Mary, and stayed with her until Hester could get there on the three-o'clock train.

I saw a lot of the Bradburys for the next three days. Hester and I felt like old friends, though we had never seen a great deal of each other, and we took a walk after supper that first night when she got back. She taught school in Franklin and now she was teaching summer school because, as she told me, the farm needed the money. She wanted desperately to be able to live on the farm herself. She was fanatic about the old times. She was married to the past, a kind of New England nun, and I knew that she would never take another husband. She felt the same need to conserve the past that I felt, but she was not compromised by Connecticut, school, and a racing bike.

While we walked in the pasture above her house, she talked about running the farm again. She thought that she and her brother Peter could make it come alive again. I said that I had heard that Peter didn't want to farm, but she wouldn't listen. She planned that they would make their own clothes and grow their own food. They would hunt and fish for meat, and find berries and nuts the woods. They would trap animals for their fur and card and spin and weave their own wool. She wanted them to live with the self-sufficiency of a Washington Woodward, not as lonely hermits in a shack, but in the old way, as a prosperous farm.

As she spoke, everything she imagined came clear to me, and I was excited, for these were old dreams of mine. Not that summer, but for many years past I had daydreamed of a self-sufficient life in the country. The Sears catalogue helped my imagining. Every summer, near the end of my time at the farm, the four pounds of the autumn edition arrived in the mail. Everyone competed to read it first. When I had been little, the long section of toys had fascinated me, and the preferences of the summer found themselves under the tree at Christmas. Later it was the pages of traps, of shotguns, of oil stoves, and of chemical toilets that I dwelled on. I made lists of the minimum requirements of a lonely trapper.

The funeral was two days later. Hester and I had been waiting for Peter, who was coming from Virginia. He came when the service was about to begin. He and Hester sat with the family in the parlor near the coffin. The minister was speaking there, and there my grandparents sat behind the family. More old people sat in the dining room, and a few latecomers stood with me in the kitchen, the third room back in the long house. It was dark, for outside it was cloudy and no one had lit the oil lamps. I heard thunder rumble far away. The kitchen was bare and harsh, where the old oilcloth gave off its special odor. All the good things of the house were gathered in the parlor with the coffin. The minister was old and his voice soft, and I only heard his voice in waves, like a radio which kept fading. The faucet rasped and the thunder came nearer, and before the sermon was done I heard the first big drops hammer on the tin roof of the shed just beyond the kitchen.

Washington Woodward was one of the old men in the kitchen with me, his stitched cap limp in his hands. I saw his mouth moving in an unvoiced harangue, even during the funeral. The others were people I recognized, but whose names I had forgotten, old faces remembered from the rear pews of the church, or from a visit in summers past in the living room of the farmhouse. When the funeral was over, I crossed to Washington Woodward and talked to him for a moment. I saw Hester and Peter come out through the kitchen, talking. They disappeared in a shed beyond us. I looked over Washington's shoulder, through the door into the dining room, where my grandparents moved among friends. Mary's sister was serving coffee. I walked away, remembering something, and Washington shifted in mid-sentence to another ear. I went back to the shed to find Hester and Peter, and I could see that they were talking earnestly. I heard her say, "You promised to stay." I backed out again.

In the kitchen I leaned on the set-tubs and watched the rain, which darkened the yard between the house and the road. The big cars moved slowly there, and the headlights showed the thick ropes of the rain. In a minute Peter rushed out of the shed and through the kitchen. His army uniform was mussed from his night on a bus, but his face looked fresh. I waited for Hester but she didn't follow him. I decided to go after her.

Her back was to me and her shoulders were shaking. I wondered whether I should speak to her. Then she turned and saw me. "Peter tells me that he won't farm," she said.

"What will you do?" I said.

"I don't know," she said.

"You could stay here," I said. "You could teach school here."

"Peter will be here," she said, "with his wife. He's getting married."

"But he's not farming?"

"He's going to make it a motel." She turned away. I touched her on the shoulder but she didn't want to be touched. She told me to go away and I went.

The next day Peter left, and I saw Hester often in the rest of the summer. While she was teaching she came home on weekends, and after summer school ended in early August she moved down to stay. She and I talked about Peter and the farm. She had no hope that he would change. He had figured that the house

itself might do for antiques. People would be taking more vacations, now that the war had ended. Everybody was buying a
car. He guessed that they'd better put in a gas pump too. He told
Hester that maybe she'd like to make up the beds at the motel or,
if they had a lunchroom, do some cooking.

We could still talk about the past, and then she became en-
thusiastic. She loved me to repeat the stories my grandfather
had told me. As for me, it seemed that I enjoyed being away
from my grandfather, and with someone only eight years older
than I. In the evening Hester and I might take a walk for an
hour. I hayed in the afternoon, but I didn't tag after my grandfather in the morning, or stay with the old people in the sitting
room at night.

Old Home Day, that summer, came shortly after the funeral.
I suppose in its nature Old Home Day is a depressing celebration, but I had never thought so when I was a child. Back in the
thirties they were held in the Methodist Camp Grounds, in the
center of a huge grove of pines. Little camps stood like dolls'
houses at the feet of the great trees, and the white church and
meeting hall loomed in the center. Every summer my grandfather and I made frequent trips to a wooden shack just outside
the grove, where huge cones of home-made vanilla ice cream
sold for five cents. The other feature of Old Home Day that
I loved was the Sanbornton Band, whose bright uniforms and
thumping bass drum made the best music I had ever heard. We
drove to the Camp Grounds in the morning, carried by Uncle
Luther in his antique car, and we ate a picnic on the pine needles at noon while the band gave us a concert. In the afternoon,
when Uncle Luther made his annual speech, and sometimes the
Governor or a Senator, I would fall asleep with my head in my
grandfather's lap.

The hurricane of 1938 blew the pines over, and the great
trees crushed the camps, the church, the meeting hall, and the
icecream stand. Soon after, the war took away the young men.
The dance in the evening ended, and the play which the young
people put on. Old Home Day became a Sunday afternoon in

August, when the old people met in the yard of a church. When Old Home Week was established by Governor Rollins in 1899, these old people had been young. It had been another Fourth of July, and the married men played the single men in baseball. The Governor had proclaimed it, however, for a reason which the years made plain. Old Home Week was the time for returning to the place you had left; even in 1899 the country was empty-ing. By 1949 most of the survivors of those who had left fifty years before didn't even know they had an old home. The orig-inal emigrants were dead or too old to travel.

Always there would be a few other children there, so that I would have someone to talk to, but mostly the old reminisced with the old. Sometimes a middle-aged woman would appear with some grown children, and the old people would stare at her while she smiled nervously. Suddenly someone would say, "Are you Abel Cuttner's daughter?" and she would say yes, and be happy to be recognized. Then she would show off her children, and the old people would look for Abel Cuttner's forehead, or long earlobes.

People who couldn't leave their houses all winter gathered strength in July for the August Sunday. On that day the old peoples' homes emptied. Each year, of course, some were dead who had come the summer before, and I heard many an old voice doubt that it would last out another winter. Hands were shaken at the end with a firmness that feared that these hands would never shake again. I stood with my grandfather while he talked to an old lady with whom he had played on a hayfield sixty-odd years before; a man with whom he had wrestled in the summer evenings after work at the hame shop; and a boy who was the grandson of the best friend of his youth, dead for forty years.

That year Hester and her mother were the center of atten-tion, because William had died only two weeks before. The old people clucked and recalled the past. No one mentioned William's twenty years of drinking and fecklessness. Hester looked haggard, but nodded her head to all of them. I found

Robert Buck, and we leaned against the side of the church and talked. All I really liked to do with him was play catch, but we didn't have a ball, and it was Sunday besides. He talked about cars, and I talked about books, until our families gathered us for the journey home.

The day I was going back to Connecticut, I was sitting in the living room quietly, when I heard noises from the dining room. My grandmother seemed to be crying, and my grandfather was soothing her. They must have thought I was outside. Then I heard my grandfather say, "Everybody changes. He's grown up now." I felt immediately guilty. I had known for a week, but never faced it, that I was happy to leave this summer, as I had never been happy before.

I went home, and went off to school. Immediately I felt nostalgic for the farm, where I could be myself and do what I wanted. I wrote my grandparents a long letter, full of my love for them and for the farm. When the answer came, it brought terrible news. Just before she had to return to teaching, Hester forced her mother to visit her sister, and locked herself in the house and burned it down around her.

TEN

LATE SUMMERS

T HE NEXT summer and the summer after, I worked in Connecticut. I visited the farm for a week between school
and job, and again between job and school. While I was there,
I joined the life of the farm as quickly as I could put on my
country clothes. I fed the chickens—my grandmother's job for
the rest of the summer—and hayed with my grandfather. At
night we listened to Gabriel Heatter and ate our snacks. Yet
everything seemed deliberately nostalgic, like Old Home Day.
I wasn't coming to hay for a summer; I was taking a vacation
where I had spent the summers of the past. My grandfather accepted the change as if he had expected it. My mother before
me had grown up and moved to the city.

Nearly everyone I knew had a summer job. They made money to spend on Saturday night or to save toward the purchase
of an old car. The real reason I stayed in Connecticut was a girl.
I was away at school most of the year and we could see each
other only in the summers. We went to parties of couples going
steady, and we danced to the music of a portable radio; there
were the beach parties and drive-in movies, and the long hours
parked in the car. The saxophones of roadhouses celebrated our
biggest occasions—birthdays, obscure anniversaries, and the un-
endurable farewells before school. On other nights we ate with
parents and looked at each other without being able to touch,
full of desperate love and the bottomless vanity of adolescence.

The winter day when I broke with my girl, and felt all the
anguish of a pain that I was responsible for, I knew that I would
spend the next summer on the farm. I would live in quietness

121

with the old, without the deliberate gaiety of the tanned couples at the summer dances. I felt a rush of relief to be rid of Connecticut, and the blocks of houses in which I had foreseen my
life. Even though I knew that the farm was only for the summer,
I took it eagerly. It was the only alternative I knew.

After my exams I spent a week in Connecticut, and then took
the train to Boston and crossed the city in a taxi and took the
Boston and Maine to Potter Place. Ansel—my cousin Edna's
husband—met me at the station with my grandmother, and the
old sedan chugged the two miles to the farm. My grandfather
was milking. Ansel beeped the horn, which sounded like the
bleat of a sheep, and my grandfather came to the window of the
barn as I had seen him do so many times. His ancient cloth cap
sat on his head against the mosquitoes, and in the cool of early
evening a light brown sweater was covering his gray work shirt.
He unclasped the broad door and came running down the hill
to hug me, while my grandmother scolded, "Wesley, the doctor
said you shouldn't run."

The first time I remember seeing my grandfather was the
September I turned four. My parents had driven north with me
from Connecticut to the farm, on my father's two-week vacation. I remember the green roadster from snapshots. My grandfather was not at the house when we drove in the yard, so after
we had kissed my grandmother we drove a hundred yards further up the road to seek him. He was calling his cattle. Usually
he hiked in the pasture to gather them, if they were late to come
down for milking, but now he was still weak from pneumonia.
He had carried his milking stool—really an old leather chair
from which he had removed the arms and the legs—onto a bare
slope, and he was sitting on it and calling up the mountain, "Ke-
bo-o-o-osh, ke-bo-o-o-o-osh." When he saw us, he picked up
the chair and ran down the hill to us, for all his weakness, and he
lifted me up and kissed me on both cheeks.

This time the three of us hugged each other in an enormous
embrace and Ansel drove away in embarrassment. My grandfather, who had already finished his dinner, went back up to the

barn to finish milking, while I settled down to a fried Spam and raw onion sandwich. My grandmother sat with me, giggling and clucking to herself, enjoying the idea that I was eating such an absurd and traditional meal. "Would you like to do chickens this summer?" she said.

She knew I would, and when I had eaten a floury cupcake, we walked up the hill to the grain shed and filled the pail. I fed the chickens with the same motions which had occupied my old summers. The June sun was still high, and Kearsarge was nearly luminous in the haze of the late afternoon heat. The cows lowed as my grandfather let them out, and I thought I could hear the distant bleat of a sheep down by the lake. We met my grandfather in the yard as we came back from the chickens. "All done?" I asked.

"All done for now," he answered, and put his arm around me. "But when the sun's up again there'll be more to do. And for you too. It's good to have a hand again." We sat rocking on the porch, without lights because of mosquitoes, and talked until it grew dark. Across the lake we heard taps played from the boys' camp. Then we heard voices coming up the dark road and soon saw two counselors—my age, I suppose—walk past on their way to the juke box down at Sabine. The man who bought Uncle Luther's house had built cabins and a snack bar.

The summer was haying and reading and writing. Letters served me for talk, and I did not miss the beach parties. The restlessness which I had felt in the racing-bike summer was satisfied now. I was twenty years old, I knew what I wanted, and my grandfather's stories seemed as fresh as ever. He was surprised when I asked him to repeat his old poems, and happy. He had remembered some more that I had never heard, and he spoke them that summer in public, at a golden wedding. Clarence and Katie Fowler, distant relatives of ours, danced and kissed and cut a cake, and Wesley spoke his pieces, just as he had done at the Lyceum fifty years before.

Except that I was older, the summer was like the ones before. We hayed the same fields and lived the same life from coffee in the morning till milk and Moxie at night. The flowers were bright in the circular bed outsïde the kitchen window, behind which Christopher sang as brightly and as rarely as he ever did. What was different was my sense that I was returning, and that my return was the choice of one life over another. None of the editors of the *Harvard Advocate* could imagine me living as I did; whatever I told them about it was understood as affectation, I am sure. When they lived in the New England countryside, they were "the city people who are wrecking the old Feebumpy place," and not the natives. Drinking beer in Cronin's in the winter, they told amusing stories about the hillbillies who were, in effect, my own people. So I was conscious of what I was doing, and sometimes it seemed like a deliberate step backward. But consciousness was good too. When I stood on the top of the hay in the sun, I contrasted it with the office where I had worn a tie for the past two summers. When I drank my milk at nine-thirty before bed, I remembered the wretchedness of love in the suburbs.

The next summer I meant to spend on the farm, but circumstances allowed me only the month of August there. August was a good time, but it was too brief and the future was too uncertain. I was graduating from college the next June, and I expected to go to the war in Korea.

One Saturday night late in November, in the middle of a gale which drenched all of New England, my grandfather had a heart attack. I went up the next week-end, and found him in bed, where he had to remain for many weeks. He was sitting up, and he told me that he felt as kinky as a barn rat. I laughed more than I would have ordinarily, and from then on, in letters and when I saw him, he always used the phrase.

Enoch Bunwell stopped continually and offered to do errands. Ansel came to milk the cows. The doctor had told my grandmother that there was no chance that he could go on milking them, feeding them, haying, or fencing. The cows had to go. Meantime they were the farm's boarders, eating up the hay that I had helped him to haul in August. A few were drying up, ready to calf in the early spring, but the new heifers would pasture on another farmer's land. My grandfather felt badly about the cows, and didn't want to talk about them.

The chickens and sheep could stay. The county workmen who cut the grass and weeds at the side of the road had made a practice of dumping some of their loads by the sheep barn, and now they guaranteed to leave enough to last the winter. My grandmother could handle the chickens and the farm could continue to seem to be a farm.

I sat beside my grandfather's bed as much as I could. Too much talking, the doctor said, would be bad for him. He was gay and full of stories, but he grew tired after a few minutes.

I visited again in the winter, when he could sit in his familiar chair in the sitting room, reading Joe Lincoln and David Harum all day long. "It's like a month of Sundays," he said. I came again in the spring, when he and I could even walk up the hill to the barn and look at the empty tie-up. For the first time in a hundred and fifty years, there were no cattle on the farm. The cows I had named as a baby, and their great-great-great-great-great-greatgreat-granddaughters whom I had known last summer, were only ghosts among the cobwebs of the old whitewashed, spiderwebbed cave. In March the trucks had come and filled themselves with the cattle, while my grandfather stood by and watched the great beasts stumble up the gangplanks, wagging the udders which his hands had stripped of a lake of milk.

There was a silence in the barn like a ruin. Nothing lived there any more. The old horse had been the last to go, a few weeks after the cows. There was still some hay up in the loft, but it would never be eaten. I wondered if the barn would burn some day, and the hay we had pitched in a distant summer go up with the old timbers. On the wall hung the harnesses of many decades, and the two pitchforks which had been ours. We walked down to the house slowly and in silence. Then my grandfather said, "It's still a good barn, if they keep the roof on her. The timber is still good." He paused. "If I was to start again, I think I would borrow money and fence Ragged with good wire and raise nothing but sheep." A moment later, I realized that he had been thinking—but couldn't say it, because he knew it would never happen; and because he didn't want me to *say* it wouldn't—of me taking over the farm after him.

It had started him thinking of sheep. I sat in the living room while he lay on the sofa and told me stories. Dogs were the curse of the sheep farmer. The state paid you for the sheep a dog killed, but it couldn't pay for the whole damage. Some sheep who hadn't been touched by a dog would just fade away and die of the terror. Others would stop bearing. One dog in one afternoon could ruin the work of a decade. Once, he remembered, he had heard crazy barking from the meadow where Uncle Luther was keeping his sheep. He got there as soon as he could, and saw a collie dog running mad among the terrified sheep, slashing and running, eating nothing, only wild to kill. He fired one barrel of his shotgun into the air in order not to hit the sheep, and then fired the other into the dog as it raced toward him. The dog leapt in the air, and ran off to die in a ditch beside the railroad tracks. Then my grandfather started to count the flock. Four sheep lay dead where he could see them, the flies already black on their torn throats. A fifth lay in a hollow. Then he climbed a hillock to see the bright eyes of a lamb watching him nervously, head held up alert, over the crest of the top. He thought, "That one looks so perky, she must be all right." But when he reached her, the flesh of one side had been torn away, and her entrails lay beside her on the ground. He loaded his gun with a shell and fired it into her head.

They were able to come to my graduation six weeks later, stiff and proud in their new clothes. I drove them back to the farm and said goodbye. A fellowship to Oxford was keeping me from the Army, and I was spending the summer in Europe. In October my grandfather had another heart attack, but the pains subsided again and in March he was well enough to celebrate their golden wedding. They sent me the photographs, and I looked at them in the dampness of my college rooms almost with strangeness. My grandmother was wearing a printed silk, and my grandfather his brown graduation suit, although he had become almost stout—the first time in seventy-seven years that he had shown any fat. All their surviving neighbors and three of their old ministers came for the wedding cake and the speeches.

That summer I returned briefly to the United States to marry the girl I had courted in my last year at college. I spent a week in New Hampshire before the wedding. Another attack in the late spring had left my grandfather quieter, but his talk was as fine as ever. He was excited to think of me marrying, and he joked about my children. Of course the doctor wouldn't let him go to the wedding, which was in New Jersey. We were sailing to England and Oxford four days later, and our honeymoon would be on board ship. We decided to drive to New Hampshire the day after the wedding, to show them the bride, and to say goodbye.

He seemed a little less stiff than he had a month earlier. It had been a good month, he said, and he felt as kinky as a barn rat. The summer was always the good time. He had thought so all his life. Obviously he dreaded the winter ahead. After supper we talked in the sitting room until nine o'clock. Then, "Time for bed, Wesley," said my grandmother.

He giggled. "Time for your bed, too?" he asked my bride and me.

"Wesley!" said my grandmother. The two old people stood up slowly and we followed them into the kitchen. The heat of the wood stove felt good in the September night. We had our late snack, and we all went to bed.

In the morning my grandmother brought us coffee in bed, shouting ahead to ask us if we wanted it, and we got up and dressed in the cold and scurried down to the warm kitchen. During the day we introduced the farm to Kirby. We walked to the two barns, and showed her the pump of clear cool water in back of the house. We passed my grandmother's playhouse, and looked at the fallen shed and the caving sap house. "I made a lot of syrup two years ago," said my grandfather. "It'll last us another year."

He paid great attention to Kirby, and told her the stories he thought she would like to hear. The day passed quickly. At twilight after our early supper, my grandfather and I walked outside while the two women washed dishes. He had been thinking about weddings, and he told me how Washington Woodward—in a youth I could hardly imagine—had tied a cowbell under an aunt's bed and rung it every ten minutes during her whole wedding night.

We walked slowly uphill to the barn, which looked like a rocky ledge of Ragged in the gray light. When we were nearly to the milk shed, he suddenly pointed upward at the branches of the great maple next to the old outhouse. "Look!" he said. "There's a hedgehog!" I followed the angle of his finger and saw what resembled a bird's nest at a fork in the branches, indistinct in the late light. "Let's see how you are with a shotgun these days," he said.

I lifted the gun from its peg where it hung in the shed nearest the kitchen. My grandfather rummaged to find a bag of shells. He hadn't fired a gun since his first attack. There were four shells with the right size shot, and one shell which fired a slug which could kill a bear at close range, but was too inaccurate for anything small. I took aim and fired the four shells of shot, one after the other. The only obvious result was the ache of my shoulder, where the kick of the gun bruised it, for though I shivered the branches around the hedgehog, I couldn't make him budge. "He's hit," said my grandfather, "but he won't fall off for you. Hedgehog will stay on a limb until you cut the limb off."

He reached for the gun. I had done all the shooting because of his heart, but now he loaded the slug into the breach, and raised the gun quickly and fired; I will never forget him raising the gun to fire it straight up, in the near darkness, puffing with the unusual effort, seventy-seven years old, and sick after a life of hard labor. The hedgehog sprang up in the air, seemed to pause there, and then fell to the ground turning slowly in the air like a huge leaf. He smiled to see what he had done, and said that he guessed he had his eye still. The next morning we said goodbye after breakfast, all of us weeping, and I never saw him again.

ELEVEN

OUT OF THE GARDEN

H E DIED in March. A letter from my father told me that my grandfather had been in bed with a cold, and had died perfectly suddenly, just after he had spoken. All spring, while the daffodils blossomed under the trees, and the poppies and the mustard took turns in the English meadows, I felt concentrated on grief. We returned to the United States in July and went to the farm to visit my grandmother. I was twenty-four years old, and my grandfather had lived to make old bones, yet my grief was unmodified. My poems were keens over the dead, glorifying him as the saint of a destroyed civilization.

That fall we went to California for a year, and in the spring our son was born. The next September we settled in New England for three years, and drove to the farm often. When Andrew was three and a half we visited there over a long week-end in October. The leaves were at their brightest in Massachusetts, but as we drove north we passed into early winter, a country of bare trees where only the oaks retained their leaves. September was the best month in New Hampshire. Even in August, red branches made flickering appearances, like fire beginning to tear through a layer of coal. The fall of 1942—when my grandfather shot Riley—I stayed at the farm late enough to see the colors. Ragged Mountain erupted in a texture of red and orange, and the hills across the valley answered it. Stark green conifers stood among the maples, elms, and oaks like guards of summer.

As I drove, I was thinking of my own visits to the farm when I was a child. I was four when I saw my grandfather sit on the hillside in the low sun and call his cows. Later, when we drove up in my father's car, I was taught to recognize the restaurant by the side of the road in western Massachusetts where my parents had stopped to heat my bottle when I was only a few months old. The summer I was nine, in 1938, I first made the trip from Connecticut by myself on the train, and crossed Boston alone in a taxi. The old Boston and Maine train which I always took from North Station was called the Peanut in New Hampshire. (Once it had been the *Pénult* and went to Montreal.) It stopped every two miles, and I became impatient: Pennacook, Franklin, Halcyon, Andover, Potter Place....Finally the old conductor who wore a handkerchief between his collar and his neck would call "Gale!" and look at me. Not many times a year did the Peanut stop at Gale, which was the railroad's name for the West Andover depot.

Outside, as the train clanked to a stop, I saw my grandfather whisper calm words into Riley's ear, while Riley stepped nervously in the shafts of the carriage. After the Peanut had tooted and begun to inch the two miles to South Danbury, I wedged my suitcase behind the seat and climbed into the old buggy. "Get up," my grandfather said, and Riley pulled us around and started the mile for the farm. The summer of talk had started already. First we passed Henry Powers's post office and store, with the gas pumps which Henry worked by hand. It closed at six, but Henry and his wife Nettie waved from the porch of their house next door. Just beyond was the huge West Andover boulder, one round stone twenty-two feet in diameter. Strange horses, when there had been strange horses on that road, had shied at the gray bulk. Further on, we passed Bradbury's farm and Whittemore's farm, and over the ridge of the hill Aunt Nannie's cottage. Then down in a hollow on the right, in the beginning twilight, we could make out the white farmhouse, with a trail of smoke coming from it, where my grandmother, who had heard the Peanut go past, was spreading honey on slices of bread to fill me up after my train trip.

I tried to tell my son about the buggy which had waited for

me at the station. He was incredulous and laughed, but he liked my story, which sounded to him like any other silly account of an animal. He had never seen a horse and buggy. I realized that my mother was able to deliver me to her past, but that I could only tell my son anecdotes.

Then we drove that mile again, only eight years since I had last done it in the buggy. The depot had been torn down, and even the road to it obliterated. Henry Powers's store was gone— carried away to another town—and Nettie was dead. Mrs. Fortune had moved and the mail was delivered by the R.F.D. man. A motel and a gas station had risen on old farm land. The Bradbury place had burned to the ground. Only my grandmother and her sheep were living on the farm we visited, and the pasture where my grandfather called his cattle was growing up with bushes and young pine.

My grandmother was sitting on the porch when we arrived, wearing a new apron, and with a light stole over her shoulders. She had been waiting there for two hours, discriminating among the cars which came over the hill toward her. She carried her greatgrandson into the kitchen and our visit began. Andrew was old enough to visit her sheep and to try to pet a lamb. He and I walked along the old fences of the grown-up pasture, where he stopped to examine peculiar rocks, and the ancient, dried flops of dead cows.

The farm was still in good shape, because my grandmother kept the roofs shingled. "If the roof goes, the barn goes," my grandfather had said. In the open shed which extended from the sheep barn, the hayrack of our summers appeared to be sinking into the straw of the chicken yard. It looked like a relic of antiquity, something preserved from the Vikings. As I fingered the thin struts of the sides, still covered with bark, I found it impossible to believe that my grandfather and I had traveled on it only seven years before.

WE TRIED, when we came to see my grandmother, to do whatever errands we could do. Since Christopher the canary was dead, there needed to be another Christopher. The place for canaries was a farm halfway up Mount Kearsarge, where a woman whom my grandmother had known in school had raised canaries in her front parlor. The woman had died two years before, but her widower and son still bred the birds. After lunch one day we drove up the side of Kearsarge, past the bleak farms of sliding fields which men had made there. The road must have been closed half the winter, it was so steep, and the houses had no protection from the wind. We could look, it seemed, up the valley to the north as far as Canada, and the washing swung on the lines in an October breeze. The further we drove, the bleaker it seemed, and when we got to the right farmhouse, which was near the end of the road, we had driven into late November. My grandmother went into the house with her cage and bought a canary from her friend's sixty-yearold son. They had talked about it over the phone, so there was nothing to do but pay the three dollars and put the frightened bird into the old cage. If he didn't sing he could be traded for one who did.

As she stepped out, the wind blew against the bird and butted it into the wires of the cage. My grandmother tried to wrap her black cloth coat around it. I opened the door and we put the cage in the front seat between us, while Christopher tried to hide in his own feathers. I started the car, but before I moved it, a very old man came around the edge of the house, bent over the two canes, and shuffled toward the car. My grandmother clucked. "Could that be Henry?"

I kept my foot on the brake, and the man kept coming. My grandmother lowered her window. "Henry," she said, "why, hello."

"Kate Wells," he said, "Kate Wells." His eyes filled with tears. My grandmother made introductions, and he looked at us, but then he turned back to her. His face was red with the wind and walking, and he panted heavily. "I was in the back parlor," he said. "Jack told me you'd come. I come slowly because of my legs."

"I didn't want to make you move, Henry."

He spoke slowly, as if he didn't want to say what he was saying. When she spoke, he listened very carefully, and he kept looking at her face as if to notice something there. "I haven't seen Kate," he said, "since Wesley and Bertha died." He paused. "Did you know Helena died, too?" My grandmother nodded. The old man turned to us. "That was my son's wife. Only a girl." He leaned on the car. "Two old men now."

"It's too cold for you in the winter, Henry, here on the mountain."

"We've got wood." He pointed to the long pile of cordwood in front of the house. "We eat store food now." He looked in at the canary. "And we have the birds to sing for us. Oh, Kate, I'll go now." He was crying and he backed away on his sticks, and my grandmother motioned me to go, and waved goodbye to him.

We said nothing on our way down Kearsarge. At the bottom I turned in a direction away from home. "Are we going for a ride?" said my grandmother, who loved rides.

"I guess so," I said. We drove through George's Mills and up the long hill to New London, past the school where Uncle Luther had studied. I stopped at a drug store and bought ice-cream cones.

Going home by another route, I noticed that the gas tank was nearly empty. I pulled into the first station I saw, and asked the attendant to fill the tank. He grinned down at me and said, "Don Hall!" Then I saw that he was Robert Buck.

I got out of the car to shake his hand, but he was covered with grease and refused. I introduced him to my wife and he talked with my grandmother. "Is this your place, Robert?" she asked. "I heard you bought a place over this way."

"Yep," said Robert. "Been here eight months now, about."

I looked around. The station was an old wooden one with two pumps, nestled among a pile of used tires and some pieces of machinery. "How does it go here?" I said.

"Pretty good," he said. "I get a lot of repair work, small stuff. Pretty good. What are you doing now?"

I told him that I was back at my college, but just writing, not teaching or studying.

"That's what you was always doing," he said. "I've got three kids now myself. You ought to come over sometime and see us."

I said we would, and we had no more to say. He filled the tank, I paid him, we said goodbye and I drove off. "Nice to see Robert," said my grandmother.

"Yes," I said. When we got back to the farm, we hung the new Christopher's cage on its hook in the kitchen, and listened for his first chirping. He didn't make a sound. Christopher—my grandmother wrote us later—didn't sing for a week.

THE NEXT day was Sunday and church. A lay preacher and a regular minister alternated Sundays; four churches made the parish, and each man took two churches each Sunday, one at eleven and one at two. The church at South Danbury was on the two-o'clock schedule and that afternoon I sat in the pew where I had spent so many Sundays. Benjamin Keneston had walked the ridge pole of that church, dousing the shingles with buckets of water, the year South Danbury burned to the ground, and the church had been saved. The pew was wooden, with pads of upholstery for comfort, of which the red cloth covering was frayed and worn away. Here I had always sat beside my grandfather, while my grandmother stayed up front at the organ which she had played more than sixty years. She was playing it today. When I was a little boy, my grandfather had kept me quiet, each Sunday all summer, by feeding me the Canada Mints which bulged the pocket of his Sunday suit.

The church was small, and at the most might have held a hundred. There were fourteen of us there: my grandmother, my wife, my son and I, the preacher, four old women seated together, and a young husband and wife and their three small children. I sat behind the hairy neck of the husband, the only other man in the congregation. His children kept squirming around to look at Andrew. For the first hymn, the lay preacher called for one I had learned as a child, and we sang:

"I come to the garden alone,
While the dew is still on the roses,
And the voice I hear
Falling on my ear,
The Son of God discloses.

As He walks with me,
And He talks with me,
And He tells me I am His own;
And the joy we share as we tarry there,
None other has ever known."

I heard, suddenly, my grandfather's tuneless voice intone the words beside me, and I turned to see him, but he was not there; only the fray of the red cloth where he had sat more than fifty years.

The first thing that struck me was the absurdity that his ghost should attempt to sing a hymn; he was conscious that he could not make a tune, and he never sang in church. Then I realized that it was I who sang, and sang tunelessly, the hymn I had loved as a child. To know the singer changed the meaning. I turned off my grandfather's voice as if it had been a radio. While the lay preacher read his stupid sermon, I tried to set in order the box of string too short to be saved, which I had kept as a miser keeps gold. The forest which I had cut down, to cultivate the land, grew up again, and the trees rose on the bare hills.

I understood that my grief, which I still carried like comfort, was not for my grandfather. The red branch on the green tree was not only the first limb of the Republic to feel the cold of the winter; it was the death of childhood, and the knowledge of my own vulnerability. It was not my death that I saw in it; what I dreaded was the end of my hermitage in a garden alone. I did not wish to acknowledge that the garden was not there. On the farm I felt myself protected by the old in a gallery of the dead. They sang that I was their own, and by answering them with elegies for the rural past I evaded the real taste of my discontent.

That past had been at least a more vital order than the order of houses in rows. The Bible in the parlor had held lists of births, baptisms, marriages, and deaths—and it held the power which sanctioned the stages of life. Yet what was real and has ceased to be real is nothing, and to value nothing is to be sentimental. The reality of the suburbs had allowed me exile in the nostalgic order of the farm. Hatred of living anarchy became love of dead order. Nostalgia was self-hatred. Yet the suburbs were no better, for being real, than they had been before I understood. I saw that I stood nowhere at all.

That night as we drank milk and Moxie before going to bed, my grandmother said that she had looked in the apple trees after church, and her late apples were eaten. Animals had plagued her all the years since my grandfather died. In the summer the deer were bold enough to come down the side of Ragged and cross the road into the garden beside the sheep barn, eating her peas and corn. The deer, who had wandered among the hills and streams for centuries, had not entered the garden for a hundred and fifty years: the brief hold of the New Hampshire farmers.

"What kind of animal?" I asked, though I knew the answer.

"Hedgehogs, I suppose," said my grandmother.

In the morning before breakfast I took my grandfather's shotgun from its pegs on the wall, where he had hung it after our night five years before. I cleaned it and loaded it with the shells which my grandmother found, shells which my uncle kept for his own gun. I walked out near the apple trees and looked up in the branches in the dawn light, and found three birds' nests against the gray sky, and fired until I brought them down. I picked up the dead hedgehogs with a shovel and carried them back, my shoulder aching from the recoil, and buried them in the garden among the graves of cats and woodchucks, and the fox I had found on the barn floor.

However many I shot, they would come back again. I felt that I could look ahead and see another year, when all the people were gone, and the gas tanks turned rust-red among the litter of fallen motels. Frost heaved the macadam, and bushes grew through the cracks in the road. While I watched, the highway grew over like the railroad tracks in the woods. The brown bears came back, hibernating in the cellars of houses. Wildcats jumped on deer from the branches of shade trees. Huge animals lumbered out of the holes where they had slept for ten thousand years.

Those animals hide under the blond hayfields of childhood.

FAMILY SNAPSHOTS

Wesley Wells and sheep.

Wesley carries sap to the sugarhouse.

Washington Woodward.

Wesley at haying time.

Wesley and Kate with their daughters.

Donald Hall on milk pail.

Wesley and Kate at time of marriage in 1902.

Aunt Alice and Uncle Luther.

Benjamin Keneston

*Wesley, at the center of the picture, ready for haying
with three horses and three helpers*

Uncle Luther.

The house of string too short to be saved.
The author's grandmother stands over the author's mother in 1904.
The dog with the baby is named Hunter; the dog at
the screen door is Trip.

Wesley in the tie up.

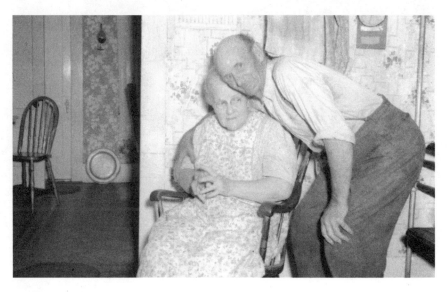

Kate and Wesley

Grandfather Wesley

Grandmother Kate, Lucy Hall, and the author's daughter, Philippa.

Donald Hall and Jane Kenyon

EPILOGUE:
MORE STRING (1979)

1. *Years Between*

WHEN *String Too Short to be Saved* appeared in 1961, the *Boston Globe* asked me to do an article about writing it. I wrote: "I was lamenting a world that I could never visit again." I quote these words here to startle myself again, as I do every day of my new life, with the reality and the joy: four years ago, I returned to the house of string; this is where I live now and forever, knowing that I will not leave except in a box, to take residence with my ancestors in the Andover graveyard.

When I lamented this world, I knew I could never live in it, and for reasons I thought unalterable. Deeper than those reasons was my conviction that the world I loved was *gone*. There were the confirmations of landscape: burnt houses, new trailers, grown-over fields; and there were deaths: Aunt Nannie was first, then Luther Keneston, Washington Woodward, and above all my grandfather, the farmer who by his labors kept the fields clear and the pastures open. I made that familiar confusion of personal loss with social decay; in the death of one man I saw the death of his people and his landscape.

Of course, I came back to see my grandmother. Every summer we loaded the car in Ann Arbor and drove east through Canada, north to Lake Erie, dipped down at Buffalo to the New York Thruway, counted the miles as the hills approached, and crossed the river into New Hampshire at the private toll bridge near Claremont. Driving to the farm in August when the *New Yorker* had published "The Blueberry Picking" (they called it "A

151

Day on Ragged"), I was so eager to arrive that I almost ran out of gas, stopping at Sturgis's gas station and general store with the needle on Empty just a quarter mile south of the farm. Don Sturgis strode toward the car with a gas pump in his hand saying, "Where *is* that blasted railroad anyway?"

Here I must confess to inventing the railroad on Ragged Mountain. (Wherever I go in New Hampshire now, I am teased about this railroad. And I have heard indirectly of two or three old timers who know *exactly* where it is, and in fact they will take you there and show it to you, but for some reason or other, they can't do it today.) As I was writing about a real day picking blueberries on Ragged, I remember how my pen ran away from me and told about a railroad that embodied my fantasy of an impossible journey into the past. And I know where the imaginary railroad came from. I have seen abandoned tracks here and there, mostly connected with an old mining industry. And when I was a small boy sitting on the porch with Uncle Luther, he told me of a walk in the woods somewhere—I don't know where—and feeling under his feet the ties of an abandoned track. Luther was an elegist too.

Little else in this book departs from the factual. I changed a few names: "Washington Woodward" was really Freeman Morrison.

WE CAME every summer to see my grandmother, who stayed healthy and vigorous and alone. She kept sheep and chickens for many years; my little children patted lambs. Her garden shrank, and year after year, she herself shrank. But at her ninetieth birthday party, at her daughter Nan's house in Tilton, she sat firm and pretty in an upright chair, scoffing at the attention she loved, snorting that she was only thirty-nine.

We stayed each summer for a few days only. I would wander through sheds and barns, showing my children the objects of old summers, paddling with them in Eagle Pond, fishing. We would then return to Ann Arbor and the life we lived there, a life of parties and schools, lectures and plays, English departments and picnics, tennis, tenure, and Volvos. Gradually that life disintegrated; my marriage fell apart. I moved to an apartment where my children visited on set days. There were six years of frustration and destruction. Through it all, like so many men and women, I held to the existence of my children, as to a raft in the ocean. But I had another raft as well. I held intact somewhere inside me the image of *one day*: the sun is high, the wind blows over the hay, my soul floats out of me into the blue air of a New Hampshire August, my grandfather mows a home field, and in the house my grandmother tends the range's fire. But this second raft was only retrospective; I lived a lamentable life.

Through all these years I took no comfort from a notion that I could return. I had given up on that; money allowed no daydreams. Every year I took the children back to the farm and my grandmother. Several times, my mother drove my grandmother to Ann Arbor late in the summer—taking three days for the drive, stopping always at Niagara Falls, which my grandmother and grandfather had wanted but failed to visit together. She sat on a porch in Ann Arbor as solidly as she sat in Wilmot, but without her apron and her chores. Then she began to be old. When she was ninety-two she fell on the farm porch and broke a small bone in her leg. She lay in a hospital for weeks; we visited, and brought Dairy Queen sundaes. She had never been ill, and this injury affected her mind, which turned childish, obsessed with small matters.

After five years of living alone I fell in love. When Jane and I were married we visited New Hampshire, where she had never been, and she loved the land, the house, and the people. Still, we did not conceive of return. I wrote a textbook which did well, and allowed us to consider moving to the country outside Ann Arbor. Jane had grown up in the country, attended a one-room school. One day we were driving north of town, idly looking at farms and farm country—when she suddenly said: Why are we thinking of *here*, when there is New Hampshire?

My grandmother had moved to the Peabody Home in Franklin, fourteen miles southeast of the farm. I spoke with my mother and her sisters, who would inherit the place. We had the land surveyed, boundaries established for the first time in more than a hundred years. We would buy the farm from my grandmother's estate when my grandmother died. She was ninety-six years old; we knew she would never return. Now my mother spent May–October at the farm, visiting her mother every day, then returned to Connecticut for the winter while the farm froze under snow. We conceived a plan: I would take a year's leave from the university, and Jane and I would live at the farm and write, keeping it warm one winter at least; we could spend the year in anticipation of living there, trying it out; perhaps I could take early retirement from teaching...

In August of 1975 we sublet our Ann Arbor house and loaded a U-Haul trailer with a year's worth of books and manuscripts, a television set, and two comfortable chairs. It was twenty-five years since I had last spent a summer haying with my grandfather. We unloaded at the farm on a fine day under Ragged Mountain, with blue Kearsarge standing forth to the south. We called on my grandmother who was silent. I think she knew that we had come to the farm. In a day or two she took a turn for the worse. I was with her when the last small breath left the ninety-seven-year-old body on August 17, 1975, and we buried her next to my grandfather on the Andover plain above the Blackwater River. It was impossible not to imagine that she had waited until we arrived to take over the old place.

In January we passed papers, but the real transfer took place earlier. I don't suppose I thought she would ever die, but when she died I knew that the place had really come to us, a life tenancy as she had taken life tenancy from July 3, 1878. In the autumn, when we had lived alone on the farm for a few weeks, it came over us that we were inheritors. My children visited from their schools, and I permitted myself to think of becoming a grandfather. We tucked the house up with leaves, insulation against snow. We lived in the constant presence of the dead that autumn. In the barn someone called Jane by name. At South

Danbury Church I saw my great grandfather alert in the pew
beside me, and I watched my grandmother's black sequined hat
bobbing over the organ she had played for seventy-six years,
from the age of sixteen to ninety-two.

There is a book to write, about coming back. I say "back,"
but I had never before spent a whole winter on the farm. Our
first January it was -36° one morning on the porch at seven
o'clock. And the *Concord Monitor* informed us that it was the
coldest January in New Hampshire's history, the records kept
a hundred years. We lived through a January colder than any
Kate had lived through, in ninety-seven Januarys. We earned
our place, carrying wood for the Glenwood stoves. Next year
when I had resigned my professorship, to live here forever,
we bought storm windows, and insulated the second story, in-
stalling small stoves in each of our studies. We keep four stoves
going now.

I thought we were coming to a house we loved. We were, and
the back chamber holds detritus of a hundred years: maybe fifty
chairs, ten double beds, twenty quilts, many tools and broken
machines, dolls and doll furniture, three spinning wheels, rusted stoves, a baby carriage, a school desk, and four highchairs. I
thought we were coming to hills and stone walls we loved—and
we were; Kearsarge and Eagle's Nest, Ragged Mountain, Eagle Pond, most tangible late in autumn, after lush summer and
spectacular autumn, leaves gone, and the shapely hills regaining
their shape, the abrupt granite visible again.

What I did not know: the people remain, we belong among
them, and they are not dead but endure. The dead are dead
enough, and their descendants occupy new bodies, but *everything
is the same.* When I was young, I could not credit the power of
place and tradition to re-embody itself. When my grandfather
died I claimed his kind was dead. Last autumn when I turned
fifty, eighteen cousins assembled at a surprise party in our living
room; and the gene pool bubbled, live faces sponsoring recol-
lection of dead photographed faces on the walls around them: a
chin here and a forehead there. But cousinship is not the matter,

for the people who live here—in old farmhouses mainly, but also in trailers, in shacks, in ranches, in A-frames—take from the dead, and from the enduring land, qualities of frankness, wit, honesty, and goodness.

2. *Being Here*

FOR THE first time I live in the present. For most of my life, I daydreamed the future: as a child I daydreamed that I would live on Ragged as a lonely trapper, and I read the Sears catalogue for supplies. When I was a professor I daydreamed sabbaticals in England. Now I daydream once a day: when I am sleepy at night I go over what I will do tomorrow. I no longer require a wished-for future to cancel the present. I am in daily touch with the past without living there. I suspect that the only present we can really live in—the only enduring present—is one that makes connections: horizontally to other people living now elsewhere under other circumstances; vertically down to the dead and up to the unborn, down to history and up with endeavor. In the Middle Ages most people lived only on the timeless and vertical plane of religion, seasonal change an endless circle: the same round between heaven and hell. Now most people live only on the horizontal, and our time is space: miles and numbers, quantities and travel. The enduring present lives at the point where these lines cross.

They cross every day. My cousin Forrest is a contractor, and with his men he jacks up our woodshed to dig out the shreds of a hundred-and-twelve-year-old sill, pour a new sill of concrete, and lower old walls back down. Joe Bouley does much of the work, with whose brothers I played baseball in the 1940's while Joe was a GI in England. Joe speaks of a surviving brother, of England, of sills, of old wood and new. Digging in the soft, fibrous soil, Joe makes continual archaeological discoveries: there are a dozen bottles, vanilla and smelling salts and spirits, handblown and eccentric and delicately colored; there is the brand K for Keneston, to tarbrand sheep after shearing; and one day in August, as new boards slap over old ones for another century, Joe brings me his best find of all: in a rusty metal lunchbox, dug from two feet down, there are several hundred clay marbles, pitted and irregular, in pastel shades of blue, pink, green, and brown, the Spanish doubloons of some unknown childhood. I wonder: could I have buried them, forty years ago...? No; for glass aggies were the treasures of the thirties. But I save them now, with my custodianship, for someone who will let them fall through fingers not yet born.

3. *Mount Kearsarge*

WE LOOK out the window at Mount Kearsarge, which stands tall and aloof, steep sides and narrow flat top, five miles to the south. In late fall it is stark and cold, bare curves accumulating pallor toward the summit. In winter it raises the glory of its whiteness, against which stand the green of fir and the harsh gray of oak trunks. When spring comes it softens overnight into pale green, and birch emerges white from the melt of snow. In summer it lords over the green morning, rising like some massy deity over the hayfields around it. Then late in August sumac on its lower slopes begins the flame of autumn, and in September red fire of sugar maple bursts out at random, among yellow smolder of birch and perpetual green pine.

Kearsarge tells the weather. For most of my grandmother's ninety-seven years she stood at the kitchen window early in the morning—beside her rocker, under her canary, in its many incarnations always named Christopher—braiding her long hair and looking out at Kearsarge. "Mountain's real pretty today," she would say to my grandfather bringing sticks for the stove, or "Can't see the mountain too good today." When clouds moved north or east to cover Kearsarge's slopes, you knew the cut hay would be wet in the summer morning; in early winter you saw the snow over Kearsarge before the first flakes fell into the brown hayfields and over the stalks of the kitchen garden.

When Benjamin Keneston moved to this farm in 1865, he had been working a hillfarm on Ragged Mountain, where the frost held back and the growing season was weeks longer than it was in the valley. But the railroad came through the valley, and with it the possibility of shipping milk to Manchester or Boston. In the valley the fields were flat, and you could grow hay for cows, and raise fieldcorn for silage. By Eagle Pond the water held back the frost—and Benjamin could look out at Kearsarge from his captain's chair on the porch. Now his face smiles out at me—with downturned mouth, skeptical and witty—from an oval frame in the sitting room, portrait taken by a photographer named Lyman Currier in Andover at the turn of the century. I have learned, since moving back here, that he loved Kearsarge, that he looked to it each morning as his daughter did—as his granddaughters did, as the current tenants do.

There are many hills for looking at. We sit on the side of Ragged, which is eight miles long. But Kearsarge has a presence denied the other hills. Farms and little towns surround Kearsarge on all sides— New London west of it, Warner south. All of us, wherever we stand to look, look out on Kearsarge, its colors shifting each day by sun's light and by season, its red beacon at night witnessing to invisible granite. All of us claim the best sight of Kearsarge. Primitive people, when they looked for the house of the gods, looked to mountains. There is no question where the god lives, if a god lives among us here. If we go to Boston for the day, or down to Cape Cod, or out to California, when we return Kearsarge is the first of home we see. We talk to it, we call it Old Blue, call it Mountain—welcome *it* back when *we* have been away.

When the Penacook returned to their winter grounds, from summer hunting up north, I know what told them they were coming home. Kearsarge is older than Indians, who arrived in New Hampshire only ten thousand years ago. The Appalachian Range buckled through the earth's crust—plates jamming—

maybe a billion years ago, before grass or squirrels or trees or daisies. At the warm seashore, only our ancestor amoebas inhabited salt pools. Then the glaciers came, extending great hoods of ice over hill and valley, topping Kearsarge like a white cowflop, crumbling its ledges and smoothing it out. They froze their way south, then melted north, then froze back again. When the glacier receded one more time, wildflowers grew on Kearsarge. Another time, small deer grazed on the tender leaves of saplings. Then Indians came, living on Sunapee's shore, and called this blue hill "Cu-Sa-Gee," as somebody spelled it in 1739. I don't know when it became Kearsarge, but I recognize those extra *r*'s. When New Hampshire natives travel cross country, they fly over the "Sierrer Nervarder" Range.

The Penacook dispersed; no one named Keneston survives: Kearsarge stays put. It has stayed put while the rest of us have come and gone—mice, reindeer, and people. It will remain— towering, diminished, enduring—when I am dead, when Jane is dead, my children and grandchildren; it will remain when people have vanished from the earth. Time elongates as I watch the old mountain. I look into fir and granite that four generations of family eyes have looked at. Sitting on the porch in my great-grandfather's captain's chair, I feel as if our eyes' gazing has braided ribbons of sight that reach from this farm to the slopes five miles away, invisible strands holding generations together, the living and dead and unborn braided together—permanent mountain attached to disappearing flesh.

AFTERWORD:
THE STORY OF STRING (2015)

I wrote *String Too Short To Be Saved* l living in an English village in 1959 and 1960. The book started, as it were, in 1945 at prep school when I wrote a free theme about chasing wild heifers with my grandfather. Summer on the farm was the passion of my adolescence. When I went off to college, those days remained at memory's center. Alone in London, late summer of 1951 on my way to Oxford, I wandered in the city of pubs and sausages thinking of haying in New Hampshire. In an English notebook I wrote about flies, spiders, and Holsteins.

Oxford took over, and in my second year I married. Next year I took a fellowship in California and my son Andrew was born. Then for three years I reveled in a fellowship that allowed me to do anything at all.

After six years of fellowship's dole, at last I had to get an honest job. What ignominy! I became an Assistant Professor of English at the University of Michigan. My chairman understood that I wanted to teach afternoons only, saving the morning for poems, but in the second term of my second year he gave me a ten a.m. class. When I reminded him of my preference he smiled sweetly and remarked, "We can't always have what we want, can we?" I accepted the appropriate rebuke. Shortly thereafter another university, many miles east, invited me to read my poems aloud, then asked me to join their staff. They offered me tenure at double my Michigan salary. And I could take leave without pay whenever I wanted. I flew back to Michigan with regret— I was making Ann Arbor friends; the Tigers and the Lions and the Pistons were only an hour away—but I knew I had to leave town. I told my chairman about the offer I could not refuse. He told me immediately that I could have whatever I wanted.

We would stay at the University of Michigan, but first we would take a year's leave without pay. (I had saved up two thousand dollars.) My wife and I would go back to England for a year, but it was too soon to return to Oxford. An English poet visiting Ann Arbor recommended the greatest house in the greatest village in England, which happened to be for rent. Thus we packed up, a baby girl to go with our five-year-old boy, and sailed to The Priory, ca. 1498, in the village of Thaxted northeast of London.

That year I reviewed books for the *New Statesman*, performed small literary tasks, and talked on BBC radio—enough so that we flew back home with two thousand dollars. Every morning I got up early and worked on poems, the habit of decades, and after Andrew left for the village school I kept up my correspondence and did chores. I watched my baby daughter nursing from breast to cup. After lunch and a nap, I retreated to the music room on the second floor of the Priory and tried to write prose. I began with a story about pursuing wild heifers.

Earlier I had written reviews and academic papers or lectures, and at first my paragraphs sounded like an English professor lecturing about the New Criticism. I required an entirely different voice to describe a cow's teats. When I showed my wife a draft of the first chapter, she prodded my style from the classroom towards New Hampshire's hay and cattle. In eighteen drafts at last I finished "The Wild Heifers" and continued in afternoons to accumulate other stories for *String*. I wondered if a magazine might publish a chapter or two. I sent "The Wild Heifers" to the *New Yorker*—they had printed my poems—and received a polite refusal. I decided this book wouldn't do for magazines. After almost a year we sailed home. The baby had moved from the breast to a heedless happy dashing to and fro. We bought a harness with a tether, in order to walk on the Cunarder's deck without losing anybody overboard.

Back in Ann Arbor I sent the manuscript of *String Too Short*

To Be Saved to the Viking Press, which had published two books of my poems. They liked it and scheduled publication in 1961. Pat MacManus, I don't forget her name, handled promotion for Viking, and sent bound galley to magazines for review, or to anyone who might take notice. Most of her pre-pub copies had left the office when she thought of sending one to E.B. White. The famous essayist had lived in Manhattan and written for the *New Yorker* (with a sideline of children's books) but was devoted to the countryside. He retired to Maine with his wife Katharine, where he continued to write impeccable prose. Then my telephone rang and it was Roger Angell, E.B. White's stepson by Katharine's first marriage, also a *New Yorker* editor and notable assistant to editor William Shawn. Roger spoke with excitement about the book his step-father mailed him. Everyone loved my stories, he told me, and the *New Yorker* wanted to publish "The Blueberry Picking" and "The Wild Heifers." He added that if they had known of these stories earlier, they would have published more. With revenge, in morbid joy, I told him that the *New Yorker* had rejected "The Wild Heifers." He looked at editorial notes and found that two editors had *liked* it but sent it back. He apologized with some chagrin, and told me never, ever, to tell anyone this story. Naturally, I have told everyone this story.

The book came out, had good reviews, and in time sold out its first printing. Viking did a second printing, which sold slowly. In 1975 I quit my Michigan professorship and with my second wife Jane Kenyon moved back to New Hampshire, to the old farm, taking my grandparents' place, freelancing instead of farming or grading papers. I noted that *String Too Short To Be Saved* was out of print. I sent a Viking copy to David Godine who redesigned it, added my epilogue, and printed it in paperback over and over again.

It was bliss to live in the house I had always wanted to live in. For decades I had thought that it was impossible; it wasn't. Jane and I freelanced, and lived here for twenty years together, writing poems in our workrooms at opposite ends of the house. In our double solitude we gazed at barn and tie-up, at Kearsarge and Ragged Mountain. In 1995 Jane died of leukemia in the bed where I still sleep. I write for both of us.

I continue to live in our place. Godine's reissue of *String Too Short To Be Saved* was always my ticket of return. When I meet a new neighbor—at the gas station, at town meeting, at the Fourth of July—I am still asked, "You the fellah wrote the book?"

A NOTE ON THE TYPE

String Too Short to Be Saved has been set in Monotype Bembo. In 1929, the Monotype Corporation recut their version, which was modeled closely on a classic Renaissance face derived from the 1495 edition of Aldus's *De Aetna*. The italic is specifically based on the flowing cursive found in the publications of the great Venetian writing master, Giovantonio Tagliente.